DANCING ON THE WAVES

ANGELA MACK

First published in Great Britain in 2000
Reprinted 2001
by Benchmark Press
Little Hatherden,
Near Andover, SP11 0HY.

Previous publications:
Outline for a Secretary (Chatto & Windus)
Continuity Girl (Chatto & Windus)
A Spanish Cookery book (Museum Press)
Fortress of the Eagles (Brockhampton Press)
Secretarial & Office Work (Batsford)
Working as a Secretary (Batsford)
The Language of Business (BBC)

**COVER: Use of Wren poster by kind permission of the Imperial
War Museum**

ISBN 0-9537674-1-8

Printed and bound in Great Britain by Henry Ling Ltd.,
The Dorset Press, Dorchester DT1 1HD

THE PHONEY PHLEET - HMS JENNY WREN
by A.P.Herbert. Published in *PUNCH* 30th December, 1942.

Progressively throughout the war
The lack of males grew more and more
Pronounced, but still Their Lordships swore
That women, though employed on shore
Should never go to sea.

In time they had to change their mind
And said, provided they could find
A warship of <u>non-lethal</u> kind
(The word was three times underlined)
There probably might be

A chance for Wrens - well, just a few,
To sail upon the deep deep blue
And, maybe, fire a gun or two -
But only dummy rounds, mark you -
Experimentally.

They found and fitted out a yacht,
Each individual rating got
A private bath - a comfy cot,
The <u>sweetest</u> cabin (all the lot
Were fitted H. and C.)

The stores were equally complete
With face creams, lipsticks, packed in neat
Containers, and (a special treat)
Bath salts on Sundays, I repeat
Real <u>bath salts</u>, issued free.

They named the ship the 'Jenny Wren'
They manned her without any men
And sent her off in August, when
The sea was fairly calm. And then
She met an enemy.

A U-boat surfaced, if you please,
Engaged in charging batteries,
The men on deck and at their ease
Sun-bathing in the gentle breeze -
The U 1403

Miss Jones, the Captain, called her crew
And said (although it was not new)
"England, my dears, expects of you
That every girl this day will do
Her duty.   Follow me."

She didn't need to form a plan
(They were three girls to every man)
She simply steamed ahead and ran
Alongside.   Then the fun began.
I think you will agree.

That as one woman's quite enough
To sink a sailor, this was rough
On Fritz.   He thought he knew his stuff
But Himmel, were these babies tough,
And he was one to three.

A boarding party - fighting fit
Went in and made short work of it.
They kicked, they pinched, they scratched, they bit,
They struck them like a direct hit.
From tons of T.N.T.

They heaved the Germans one by one
Aboard their ship, and every Hun
Was welcomed by a Wren - with gun -
Who knocked him down in girlish fun
Most efficaciously.

When all were safely stowed below
They took the submarine in tow
And set a course for Plymouth Hoe.
Miss Jones said "Splice the Mainbrace", so
They all had extra tea.

And that was the first action fought
By Wrens.   When they returned to port
The First Sea Lord - a decent sort -
Turned out to cheer them.   And he brought
Miss Jones the D.S.C.

Reproduced by kind permission of A.P.Watt on behalf of Crystal Hale
and Jocelyn Herbert.

INTRODUCTION

At the end of 1993 the Women's Royal Naval Service ceased to exist and overnight women became part of the Royal Navy. The reasons for this change can be argued as partly economic - one organisation instead of two - and partly the result of pressure from the equal opportunity laws. There were many heated arguments for and against but in the end a group of people, incognito behind a government arras, decided to annul the W.R.N.S and declare the navy unisex. Despite the admonitions that we must move with the times, those of us who were Wrens in the Second World War are somewhat puzzled by the new service.

There is a paradox here. It would seem that we should be delighted. The Wrens have always been an integrated part of the Royal Navy and proud of it. The one thing that we as war-time Wrens wanted to do was to get on board a ship. Some of us achieved this for such jobs as routine inspections and maintenance of artillery, checking signal books, delivering mail, etc., and, the big exception, crossing the Atlantic on the troop-carrying ships as signals personnel. Because we were needed, we succeeded in demonstrating that we could be useful and I suppose to some degree we blazed the trail.

Has the pendulum now swung too far?

By some accounts, sending Wrens to sea has not altogether been a success. The "no touching" rule is a problem. Restrict men and women to a confined space and anyone with a spark of life is likely to get attracted to a member of the opposite sex. Many women now serving in the Royal Navy say that on most ships there is no problem but others tell of bullying and the inadequacy of the women's quarters.

This is not a history of the Wrens in war-time - that has been extensively written - this is an account of how one woman saw it. How we as women thought before the war and how we felt after it seemed worth recording, especially because the WRNS as we knew it has ceased to exist. Before it all gets forgotten, this is how it was then.

1.

It is strange but among anniversaries "fifty years' ago" has an important ring about it, "sixty" even better. Those of us who volunteered to join the Women's Royal Naval Service nearly sixty years' ago can now be bold and come out of our burrows. Most of us have put up with years of being told to shut up about our wartime adventures but with the thought of the next anniversary and the demise of the Wrens as we knew it, there's a different feeling abroad. It seems that those war years have become history, written about in books and studied for exams. We are quite respectable after all.

The first difficulty in writing about the period is to get across the dramatic difference between the way we lived and thought before the war compared to our manner of thinking today. The change in attitudes is extraordinary, hard to visualise from today's outlook on life, and particularly hard for anyone under forty to fathom.

There is no doubt that Hitler's war changed the lives of everyone, but women in particular had opportunities offered to them which released them from what was, from the present viewpoint, really unbelievable restriction. There have always been the gallant rebels throughout history who refused the secondary roles they were supposed to play, but it was not until the first World War that the stepping stones were laid for real careers for women. Many women's movements began between the wars but it was not until the '39-'45 war that women, at last, got their mass release. As I was part of this, I wondered how and when, or even if, I had appreciated what was happening at the time or whether, like a cheerful gaderene, I just went with the crowd.

To set the scene: in 1939 I was growing up, like the majority of middling middle-class girls, in a cosy cocoon. We were set in the mould of our mothers and grandmothers who had obeyed their parents totally until they married, only to find, very often, that they had exchanged one household controller for another. I remember my grandmother expounding on the importance of a woman having her own money and not being completely dependent on her husband "to ask if she could buy a pocket handkerchief". She had been frantic to have her own career but at the turn of the century, few did. My mother was less adventurous: with five children she reckoned she had a career.

We lived in a suburb of London. With our parents there were six of us, soon to be seven, packed into a small house which my mother considered was spiritually part of Hampstead, with its literary and artistic connections, although geographically there was no argument: we *were* closer to the comedians' favourite joke place, Golders Green. The bad thing about the Hampstead Garden Suburb was that buses were not allowed, which meant you had to bicycle or walk everywhere. The good thing was the Heath.

When war started, our private playground, as we considered the Heath, was partly taken over for self defence. A huge balloon was installed and we spent some out-of-school time watching the problems the personnel had to get it airborne. On bad days it played hard to please and collapsed in a grey muddle of billowing uncontrollable folds. On good days it sailed aloft in an unmenacing way. It was hard to imagine it posed much threat to German aircraft. It looked to us like a friendly, floating elephant. Later a gun emplacement was built near the pond where we had caught tadpoles. As this was "our" pond, so the anti-aircraft gun became "our" gun. It made a frightening, ear-cracking CRASH-FHRUMPH when it loosed off. If we had to get up in the middle of the night, as happened frequently when Moaning Minnie, the warning siren, wailed, we would encourage our gun as soon as we heard the sound of droning German raiding aircraft overhead, with shouts of "Get the B's". We had been restrained by my father from using words like Bastards or Buggers, which was a pity as it took some of the force out of it.

If the night raids went on for a long time, we had to bring our bedding downstairs - and what my mother called an "Escape Bag" with a change of underclothes, a warm sweater and one favourite toy - and sleep against an inner wall, under the stairs, or under the stout oak dining-table. In the morning we had to hump everything upstairs again, mattresses and all. Unlike some families, who sensibly brought the upstairs downstairs, our mother preferred total normality. She did not consider that her life should be too much disturbed by a raving housepainter. She had, in fact, rather upset the bustling lady volunteer who arrived one day with our issue of gas masks. We duly tried on the rubber monstrosities, breathed out and made a rude noise to prove they were working and were given little cardboard boxes, like the foxes, to keep them in. When it came to our mother's turn she said 'No, I won't try it on now, thank you, I've just had my hair done.'

In the morning after the raids, if not a school day, we went in search of the misshapen pieces of metal known as "flak" which fell all over the Heath and nearby streets. These my father did up in small parcels and posted to Boston, USA, for his sister to sell to raise money for what was warmly called "Bundles for Britain". This aunt was a legendary person to us. She was over six foot tall, red-haired, dynamic *and* she had married a millionaire, a real one, in the 1920's, in a splendid chorus-to-riches romance. At this point in the war, 1940, there was no way of tapping the wires of the future to tell me that I would cross the Atlantic, on duty, entirely at the nation's expense and spend an Aladdin's cave visit to *her.* Aunt Ellice had defied her conventional family by going on the stage. She was much too tall for all the titchy leading men of the day . . . she said . . . but she managed to make the high-kicking heights of the West End. Her future husband saw her in a popular musical when on a business trip to London and thereafter took a seat out front and sent round two dozen red roses *every night* to her dressing-room. Since he was a formal member of Boston high society, he searched around until he found a mutual friend to introduce him. The Endicott family were of the breed who spoke only to those very near God and our ebullient Aunt had some problems getting accepted by Boston society after her marriage, but she made it. She was highly unstoppable anywhere. We had been told that she was coming home late from the theatre one evening when she was menaced by a gang of young thugs. She immediately attacked them with her umbrella and shouted at the top of a powerful contralto. The gang ran.

3

I look back with distaste at me at the time: a too-tall, self-centred schoolgirl. I visualised myself, of course, as a romantic heroine of the Georgette Heyer variety, on the look-out for Lord Worth or one of those dashing Regency heroes of that ilk. Our parents were indulgent and loving as we clashed our various egos in endless conflicts and fought over whether to splurge or eke out our butter ration, which seemed to be about the size of the indiarubber we were issued with at school. We were still children living in the age of obedience, but, looking back, it was a feather-bed existence.

My one painful childhood memory was of scarlet, swollen, itching chilblains that made November to April the season of dread. Our house was exceedingly cold. The cry-of-the-day was "Shut the door!" or "Were you born in a barn?" as a carefully nurtured huff-up, a fire-hugging fug was blasted apart by a draught to cut you in two. The British, then, believed that to have proper heating in winter was something the Americans indulged in, a slightly wicked and definitely unhealthy luxury.

The time came when I had to join something. Everyone was joining things to help the war. From the fall of France in May 1940 until the Americans entered the conflict in December 1941, the only defiance to Nazi ambitions was Britain and the Dominions. Britain was frighteningly unprepared and unorganised for such a David and Goliath contest. Everything that made up British peace-time civilian life had to be laid aside while the entire population were guided, pushed, assisted and kicked into changing gear and turning themselves into a war machine. The strains were apparent but with some painful grinding an extraordinary change of scene was taking place. Women were now in demand; out of extreme need there burst into life an untapped source of brain and skill effectively ignored since Boadicea. In the first World War, and up until this time, women had carried out the more traditional female work as cooks, drivers, secretaries and nurses. Suddenly there were a great number of important jobs and not enough men to do them. Born of necessity, women at last had the chance to break through the male sound barrier. Away from home a lot of women discovered that they had a brain and a pair of feet. As they began to use the first and stand on the second there dawned a realisation that all was not fair in terms of legislation and attitudes.   There were too many closed doors.   It was a rewarding role to be a cradle-rocker but not quite so interesting to be the power *behind* the throne.   It was not thought at that time that a woman might again be on the throne and much less that a woman could be Prime Minister - the idea would have caused as much ridicule then as it would today in Riyadh.

There was one small problem: had I any skills to offer the war effort and would one of the women's services have me if I volunteered?   Both my brothers helpfully considered the whole notion laughable, as brothers are wont to do on the no-hero-to-your-siblings principle.   My mother told me to apply to join the Women's Royal Naval Service.

It seemed a good idea.   Her reasons were not that the Navy was the Senior Service, or for any secret love of the sea but because she thought, with my father ex-army, I might prefer the A.T.S. (Auxiliary Territorial Service).   She was against this because she considered khaki an unbecoming colour for a woman.   So, when the day came for my interview, she packed me off in a floppy and unmanageable Ascot-type hat and a Liberty silk dress.   The hat elastic at the back was uncomfortable but the thought of defying her and taking the horrible thing off never occurred to me.

The Wren Headquarters was in the feminine-sounding Queen Anne's Mansions.   It was a huge building of dirty cream paint or dirty green paint and rather bleak and forbidding.   In the waiting-room was a large poster JOIN THE WRNS AND FREE A MAN FOR THE FLEET.   It seemed an admirable plan, if they would have me, but I had to face the fact, sitting on a rather hard wooden chair, with the back slat designed for a smaller back - or possibly it had been *intended* to make you sit up straight like a Victorian - I had to face the fact that I had very little to offer the Lords of the Admiralty in terms of skill or experience.

And looking at the other candidates sitting round the room I saw that they all looked competent, with darkish suits or dresses - almost in uniform already - AND NO ONE HAD A HAT.

5

2.

Names were called. The person on the seat nearest the door in the far corner of the room got up and disappeared. All the rest of us moved up one. The tension grew the nearer we got to that door. No-one came back in again. Meat in and sausages out? What happened in between?

For comfort I thought about Emma Hamilton. Would she have joined the Wrens if there had been the chance then - would she have managed to get herself a compassionate posting near Lord Nelson? As she was a remarkable woman in an emergency I felt somehow that she would. I remembered the account of how she had coped with getting the hysterical Neapolitan royal family out of their palace and into the safety of a British ship when threatened by Napoleon's invasion. She had nursed a dying baby princess, fixed up quarters for everyone and calmed nerves and arranged food while her husband, Sir William Hamilton, Ambassador to Naples, had been a tower of uselessness. He sat in his assigned cabin nursing a loaded pistol and saying he didn't want to drown with the "guggle-uggle" of water in his throat. Extremely helpful. No doubt he was thinking sadly of his collection of Greek and Roman treasures, which he had despatched home to England in two ships, going straight to the bottom, which, in fact, one of them did.

On the last chair my knees developed a wobble. "Breathe deeply if alarmed," my father had once said. I did so loudly, which made the next girl turn round in surprise. None of us spoke - I suppose we were all much too scared.

Through the door was a very small office, a table, a Wren officer looking smart and two chairs. I sat on the vacant one. It was exactly like going to see one's headmistress; but I was cheered by a flower in a blue vase on the bare wooden table. It was a bit of panache in rather bleak surroundings.

'What can you do?' was the question I dreaded. It came almost immediately. I had taught myself to type and that, alas, was a mistake.

'I'll put you down for SDO.'

'Wha . .? I beg your pardon.'

6

'Signals Distribution Office,' she said.   I had hoped for the romantic-sounding Boat's Crew at least.   I dared to ask.

'You have to have experience in handling boats . . .   A driver?   You have to have had a clean licence for at least six months.'   She looked at me as if she thought this would be unlikely.   It was all the fault of the Liberty silk.   Now . . . etc. . . she had lots of others to see.   I was dismissed and shown the other door.   I did not dare to ask if I had been accepted or not.

Three weeks' later a buff envelope arrived informing me that I should present myself for probationary training of fourteen days' duration.   If not discharged at my own request or at the discretion of the WRNS (which sounded sinister) I should then go for training as a teleprinter operator *if* I passed all the tests.

A list of "Clothes etc required by Probationary Wrens Entering for Training in the WRNS Depot" was included. Among other items was 1 rug or coloured blanket, 1 torch, 1 pair bedroom slippers suitable for hard wear (what was this for, escaping in the middle of the night?) and 2 pairs dark bloomers. These, I learned in time, were known as "closed at the knees" officially, with lots of other rude names.   No problem.   We had had to wear these outstandingly unglamorous elasticated articles at school for dashing about the gym.   Stapled to the bottom of the list was a note to say "The above requirements are desirable for Pro-Wrens, but it must be clearly understood that it is not necessary to expend coupons, or go to the expense of buying new articles."   Their Ladyships by this time must have appreciated that the exigencies of clothes rationing would not stretch to much;   also, I imagine, they had realised that women were joining from different backgrounds and different incomes. The list really implied, be sensible, bring what you can.

The first hurdle was a medical.   Another buff envelope arrived with a card telling me to report to a Doctor in Highgate at 3.30 p.m. on the following Thursday.   On arrival I was given a white overall to put on over knickers and bra.   I sat on the doctor's prickly sofa staring at his rather bull-dog shaped back.

'What illnesses have you had?'

'Measles.'   It seemed a bit of a poor show so I added 'and flu.'   The doctor laughed.

He listened to my chest with the three-way device.   He poked the suction bit at me in a haphazard hopeful sort of way as if he didn't really know what he was looking for.   I wondered what would happen in his ears if my tummy echoed like the Duchess whose rumblings abdominal were so phenomenal.   But he turned me round and thumped my back with a crooked finger. Then he went back to his desk to fill in the form.

'It says here: "are you subject to epileptic fits, heart attacks, etc. etc. etc."   Well, no I suppose?'

I didn't speak.

'How many teeth have you got?'

'I haven't any idea, I'm afraid.'   It seemed a rather stupid question.   'How many teeth should I have?'

'I haven't any idea either,' he said, 'but I expect you're all complete.'

He signed the paper and we shook hands.   The doctor obviously believed in backing his hunches and was no doubt very busy with all his proper patients.

The appointed day came and off I went to war, at tea-time, never having been anywhere very much unaccompanied by parents or my grandmother - the restrictive mode of the day in many families.   I had never even been away to school.

The probationary training depot to which I had been told to report was not very far from home.   It was a large building in Finchley Road which had once been a seminary.   It looked very plain and well scrubbed.   I wondered who did the scrubbing?

3.

It must have been the same for most of us, starting out on an adventure that would lead goodness knew where. I doubt if we even considered that this adventure might mean getting our toes through a door marked Men Only, Keep Out. The opportunity to do an interesting war-time job was the main objective. We stepped ahead eagerly, not knowing what to expect and greatly protected by innocence and naivety. But I suspect a lot of us had to go through the initial shock of actually leaving home and everyone we knew, which particularly applied to the over-protected ones like me.

The emotions of the first day come back clearly. Waking early there was a moment of panic. Outside our front door at home was a short garden path between the rose beds to the gate. Beyond the gate loomed a silence, awesome, a horrid threat to peace of mind. Suppose it was all going to be awful? Suppose they wouldn't have me at the end of the fourteen days? I couldn't see myself being any use in the Land Army, and making munitions meant standing all day; with my long back standing for long was painful. Behind all these preoccupations was the fear of leaving the family, the world outside the gate had suddenly become too alien to face. I almost wished I *had* been sent away to school. If I had I would presumably have got through these waves of advance homesickness that were like a physical illness for which there were no pills.

When the time came to leave there was a crescendo of grief. As a family we enjoy our emotions. In later years, when there were five of us coming and going, from leave, from boarding school and other adventures, our leave-takings and arrivals were so highly charged with noisy demonstrations that a neighbour opposite asked my mother if we were partly Italian. She seemed disappointed to be told that we had no such justification for histrionics. But that day the hugs and partly suppressed tears were wonderful, cathartic.

At the moment of actually leaving, I sat beside my father in the car quite exhausted but *used up* and therefore ceasing to think of anything except practical details like - had I packed all

9

the things I had been told to bring? Would their eminences think I was properly dressed in my skirt and jacket? My father had a little extra petrol owing to his position as head of a Home Guard Mobile Platoon, and as he was only taking me a few miles away to Finchley Road he decided it was a worthy cause. We kissed goodbye outside the building and I ran. I turned to watch him drive away, and although I told myself that this might be my last view of him and I had better look long, these thoughts were inevitable war-time thoughts and I was used to them. School journeys every day, visits anywhere, made everyone ponder soberly. We had had two years of fear when it was very possible to return home to find . . . nothing . . . an ugly hole where a house had been, fire hoses blocking the street and the smell of plaster and cordite. My prayers were for the family to be kept safe. That I might be the one to be hit by a bomb did not cause me much concern. I doubted it would happen, with a cheerful confidence in survival that is the right of unsophisticated, healthy youth.

Inside there were other new arrivals, looking as strained and anxious as I felt. In the echoing uncarpeted hall a Wren officer sat at a desk ticking off names. She assigned me to a very small room with six double bunks in it and I was told to unpack. All the bunks had blue and white covers, each with a blue anchor prominent in the centre - and very exactly centred they all were. We had one drawer, and hanging space for three items each. When everyone arrived it was going to be a crush. Three girls burst in soon after me who all knew each other and they were poised, self-assured and helped themselves to the top bunks.

'That's mine,'I said firmly. 'Sorry, I got here first.'

'Oh, if you're going to be like *that* . . .'

'I have to be on the top bunk as I'm claustrophobic,' said a dark girl of sophisticated mien. If she thought I was going to offer to change with her she was mistaken. I continued unpacking and placed my small bear on the bunk to make ownership crystal clear.

'Oh well, change with me, Lucinda. I don't mind a bottom bunk,' said one of the other three, with a despising glance at me, and they began talking about the course which they seemed to have heard about from mutual friends.

'My dear, I'm dreading the drill. Isn't it absurd? Making us march about like men. Too ridiculous. Lucy told me you have "parade" every morning and they put bad marks against you if you make mistakes. It all counts, everything you do is noted.'

'I thought that was on the officers' training course, how you wield your knife and fork, that sort of thing. Surely not here?'

'Well, they fail a lot, you know. There are piles of tests to pass. I'm terrified.'

'*I'm* dreading the scrubbing. We all have to scrub floors. I can't see the point. Degrading really.'

I exchanged glances with a girl who had taken possession of the last bunk of the six, underneath mine.

Under cover of all the chat and the chaos of six people in a very small space trying to unpack, the "sorry's" and "excuse me's" as we fell over each other, the girl said 'I quite like scrubbing.' She had a cheerful, no-nonsense face with a humorous expression and slightly pointed ears like an elf's.

'So do I,' I said. Actually I had never scrubbed anything but the idea was interesting. I liked cleaning and was pleased with the reputation my mother had cunningly fostered by saying I was the only one who cleaned the bath properly - when I remembered to do it. I did not see how cleaning could be degrading. Had these women housefuls of servants who did everything for them?

'Where are you from?' I asked one of the "gang".

'Shropshire,' she said shortly. 'Is your father Navy?'

'No.'

'Mine's RNVR' she said proudly. '*Her* father,' gesturing towards the one who seemed to be known as Freddie, 'is a Captain RN.' She left a pause for me to curtsey but I raised an eyebrow. Absurd really. My house is bigger than yours sort of assertion and here we were, late teens and possibly early twenties by the looks of us. It was more like primary school.

'What do we do now?'

'We "report" downstairs again, I think.'

'Don't leave your bear on the bed in case there's an inspection,' the girl who had arrived last but one said kindly to me 'or it'll be confiscated.'

'Thanks,' I said, and hid him under the pillow.

The Wren Officer at the desk said we were all free to do what we liked until nine-thirty that evening. It was now six o'clock. I rang the family and broke the news that they hadn't, in fact, got rid of me. I had ample time to catch a bus home and I proposed to join them for dinner.

This was excellent comic relief. After all the emotion of parting, here I was again. I was much teased. But the tension had been released and our final farewells later that evening were more mature on my part; I felt much more cheerful and mattter-of-fact. The sting had been taken out of the goodbye business - we'd been through it all already.

My father called out, when he dropped me for the second time in Finchley Road 'Ring us up if you want to come home for breakfast.'

4.

Looking back, I'm sure that most of us newcomers hoping to become members of the Women's Royal Naval Service were clear about one thing and that was that we were feminine creatures putting our normal lives on one side to help with the war effort. I don't remember that we thought much about "freedom of opportunity" or the chance at last to show men what stuff we were made of. But we were liquorice allsorts and others may remember differently. There were certainly a few, but only a few, who enjoyed the idea of being male impersonators. These psuedo macho characters sported Eton-cropped hair and enjoyed giving out crisp orders and relished prancing about on the parade ground.

I did not, knowingly, meet a single Lesbian; not, I think, because we did not know they existed - I certainly did not - but because I suspect that there were very few. You could argue that if you don't know Lesbianism exists you are unlikely to encounter it. However, there was never any behaviour of any sort in any of the establishments that I was in, packed full of women, organised and run by women, that gave me any suspicions. I am sure that even an innocent like myself would have noticed if anyone had acted in any way out of the ordinary. Perhaps this was just chance, or I was too horrible to merit a pass. Ignorance, chance or unworthiness, the advantage was the freedom from embarrassment, since friendships between women could exist without any tiresome undercurrents.

However this whole feminine business needs to be put in the context of the time. At that period, women were inevitably under the influence of parents and grandparents who, despite the changes brought about by the first world war and the twenties, were still well pickled in Victorian values. I suspect most of us had been subjected to the propaganda of the rustling skirt and flirting fan brigade, alive and flourishing, who remembered their youth: the handsome cabs, the dance programmes with tassle and pencil, the maid to open the front door. The two powerful women in my life, my mother and grandmother, had always been there, like guardians at either side of the gate of knowledge of life. Quite wittily and rather too often they repeated what they

13

had been told about women's wiles and manoeuvres. Their formula was simple: you had to do your best to be charming and good-natured and the world, run by men, would open like an oyster and, with luck, a splendid male would offer you the pearl ie: a proposal of marriage. Then it would be happy ever after.

So there most of us were, products of our age, pre-pill, quite pleased with being women most of the time and only occasionally fed up that men often seemed to get the best of things. We had our little resentments; for example, why was I not allowed to go out when I wished, where I wished, as my brothers were allowed to do? Why were we, my mother, sister and I, assumed to be in charge of the washing-up unless my father made a fuss and insisted the two boys did their share? There seemed little point in questioning the status quo - the men earn the money, the women look after the home; basic and uncomplicated, our roles were fixed.

A feminine object we had been instructed to bring with us was a "hussif". This was an oblong strip of material with pockets for cottons, scissors and needles, rolled up and tied with tapes. My grandmother, queen of scissors and thread, had prepared mine for me in navy blue "crash" lined with turquoise blue silk. Hating all sewing, I regarded it as a piece of equipment which I despised, it was a tiresome reminder that women were the wielders of needles. Later, when I discovered that the hussif has been part of any sailor's kit since the beginning of the Navy, I became reconciled to my hussif.

Any thoughts we might have had of becoming real sea-going sailors were banished by the rather severe motto of the Wrens "Never at Sea". I wonder who chose it? We would just have to try and live up to it in its figurative sense, although for me I felt the motto should have been "All at Sea". In due course, however, this motto in its literal sense became inappropriate when Wrens *did* take on duties afloat, including me.

But first there were fearful hurdles to leap over before we could think of ourselves as sailors, even shore-based ones. We were now faced with this fortnight of mental and physical tests and who knew what psychological assessments. We were all very nervous.

On Monday morning we assembled.

'Ladies,' said the Third Officer in her smart doeskin uniform and enviable blue stripe on her sleeve, 'you are here as Probationary Wrens for a fortnight. If at the end of that time you do not wish to join the ranks of the Women's Royal Naval Service you are free to go; and if we, on our side, consider that you do not suit us, well . . .' She was young and quite pretty and she smiled, implying that this last statement could not apply to us. I am sure the entire bunch of us smiled back.

The classes began. We rushed about from room to room taking notes on vital information such as ranks, who was who in the Service and what, for example, a blue anchor on the sleeve meant (a Leading Wren - which seemed an elevation beyond all hope of gaining) and the difference between a Rear and a Vice-Admiral. We had to adapt quickly to seamanlike language, since the solid Hampstead building had mysteriously turned into a ship. Our rooms were *cabins*, the floors *decks*; our rather odd-shaped dining-room, with its huge window of Victorian coloured glass, was the *mess deck*, and the room we would be moved to if any of us were ill was *the Sick Bay*. Our free time was *Make and Mend* - this was from 1800 to 1900. No-one knew the 24-hour clock in those days and this we had to hurry to memorise until someone kindly pointed out that from 1300 on you deduct two.

Port and Starboard were familiar to me, fore and aft were obvious, but which was the stem and which the stern? One of the lecturers was a naval officer with a beard and a proper sea-dog appearance. It must have been from him that we learnt the jolly verse of rudimentary seamanship - in case we should at any time find ourselves at the helm despite our non-sea-going motto?

> Green to green, red to red
> Perfect safety, go ahead.
> But if to your starboard red appear
> T'is your duty to keep clear.

The mixture we were given was heady stuff. A clever combination of the factual and the romantic, quite enough to send the pulse racing of any devotee of the sea. We learnt a lot of less exciting facts, too: discipline, including punishments for wrongdoing, our rights if we had to be discharged on medical grounds and grades of pay for each rank. If we passed and were enrolled as Wrens we would earn the handsome sum of £1. 0s. 11d per week, from which 5d (five pence) was deducted quarterly towards the cost of Health Insurance and Pensions. Dutifully we all scribbled in our notebooks.

One very fierce Naval officer lectured us on the terrible penalties of breaking the Secrets Act to which, when, or if, we became full members of the Senior Service we should automatically be bound. He made it very clear that it was our duty to defend our country to the nth degree, if necessary to our last breath. We were exhorted to give one hundred and twenty per cent of our best every moment of every day to live up to the great tradition of the Royal Navy. Much was made of the fact that we would be *part* of the Navy and not an auxiliary service as were the ATS and WAAF. Whatever happened we must not let the Navy down which had so generously - perhaps this particular officer secretly considered *unwisely* - allowed women to share their duties and responsibilities. Although I appreciated his unspoken reservation, it did not detract from the patriotic fervour all these talks had brought out in us. It was the "England Expects . . ." message and, I imagine, as one woman, we all gave our hearts to the Royal Navy from that moment.

Patriotic feelings were running high everywhere. At that time the war involved a considerable part of the entire world. In Europe, Great Britain seemed like a tiny fish swimming dangerously near the jaws of a huge German shark. Germany had occupied the Netherlands, Belgium, part of France (Vichy was in theory independent until November 1942), and had conquered or had allied itself to every country in Eastern Europe except neutral Turkey. Sweden and Switzerland alone were neutral in the rest of Europe. The German invasion of the USSR had begun in June 1941 and by Spring 1942 the Germans were almost at the fullest extent of their penetration into Russian territory. But Great Britain and her Dominions were no longer alone in defying this menace. Pearl Harbour had been attacked on 7th December, 1941 and Hitler declared war on the United States on 11th December. By April 1942, the pent-up weight of

16

American enthusiasm and sympathy for Britain's stand had turned into a stream of men and materials coming eastwards to throw in their lot with ours.

The campaign in North Africa was at that time out of the main news. Rommel was planning his two-pronged attack to get the British Army out of Egypt, while the British Army, under Auchinleck, was making good the losses from the recent retreat. They were also planning the counterattack. But Rommel marched in May and the Eighth Army had to withdraw from the Gazala line towards Tobruk, which was abandoned on June 21st, the army drawing back to the defensive position of El Alamein. It was not until August of that year that Montgomery took over as Army Commander.

The mood in Britain, as I remember, was one of cautious optimism and unshakeable determination. At home we had tuned in occasionally to hear Lord Haw-Haw broadcasting from Germany, doing his best to curdle every British stomach with his warnings of devastating raids and horrid threats of our impending doom. I wonder now how he would have reacted if he had been able to see into so many British homes where he was mocked and imitated, as much a source of merriment as Tommy Handley. Hitler, too, was the origin of a thousand jokes, with a finger held under the nose to represent the little black toothbrush moustache.

Luckily we did not yet know about flying bombs - the VI's and V2's. Although ignorance of what might happen makes life a lot easier, the day-to-day reaction to Hitler played its well-acknowledged part in the war effort, the note of cocky defiance sounded by Winston Churchill suited the British character. When it failed in individual cases, which of course it did, the depressed, the panickers, the fearful were shamed by the majority into keeping their gloom to themselves.

We had all been through gloom and fear. My father had thought, on September 3rd, 1939, that Hitler might invade England at once. We were on a family holiday in Bognor when Chamberlain announced over our art deco radio that Britain was at war. My father decided that the Bognor beach was defenceless and that with invasion a possibility we might not be able to return home as the roads would be blocked with tanks and troops.   The Sunday joint was removed from the oven and wrapped in layers of newspaper while we threw our belongings into the large Victorian trunk which went on the roof of our car. We were sad to say goodbye to the sea but it was all very exciting.   We handed the key of the rather stuffy little house back to the agents.   There was no question of Drake and his bowls about us.   My father later joined the Local Defence Volunteers on the day the recruiting stations opened and he subsequently got down to planning street fighting exercises.   He was a realist.   If the Germans landed, how could we stop those tanks and guns and men who had roared into Czechoslovakia and Poland, Holland, Belgium and France?   He decided that his family had better learn how we could, if it came to it, take a German out.   He showed us how to garotte the Hun with a tin hat, aim for the balls and blind them with one quick thrust of the extended fingers.   I revelled in the idea of reducing the number of the enemy by one but of course you wouldn't have seen me for dust if a German had appeared   However, I believe the psychological effect was powerful.

Now there was a chance to play a real part in helping to defeat the enemy.

5.

Despite the snippets of information on our course about how the WRNS had come about, the real story was not told to us. We had to wait until after the war when it was recounted by the person chiefly concerned: Dame Vera Laughton Matthews, DBE, the head of the WRNS, in her book "Blue Tapestry". As would-be recruits we did not appreciate the day-to-day struggle which, since 1939, had gone on behind the scenes to create an efficient group of women, dedicated to excellence but holding to an ideal that women were not neutered creatures aping men. The guidelines had to be set from the top.

The story began in 1914. When war started Vera Laughton, daughter of a Navy historian, went at once to the Admiralty on her own initiative to see if there was any job at all that she could do. She was brusquely told 'We want no petticoats here'. By 1917, however, the war casualties were so great that help *was* needed and an advertisement was published in the Times on November 29th, 1917 calling for women to be "employed on various duties on shore hitherto performed by naval ratings". Miss Laughton applied the same day and was soon put in charge of recruitment and training at the old Crystal Palace in South London. At the end of the war the Women's Royal Naval Service was disbanded, but they had numbered seven thousand at their peak and Miss Laughton received an MBE for her work for the organisation.

When the second war started, Vera Laughton Matthews, as she had become, was summoned to the Admiralty in February 1939 to attend an Advisory Committee to discuss the re-formation of the service, attended by, among others, the Head of Civil Establishments, Branch I, a Mr. LeMaitre. In her book, Vera Laughton Matthews gives Mr. LeMaitre the credit for officialising the word "wren" for the individual members of the new service, who were to be "limited to those who lived near enough to a Naval Port to be able to attend for training . . .": an interesting beginning, indicating that the original recruitment was visualised as quite small. A short time afterwards she was called by telephone to be interviewed for the post of director, as

19

she believed. On arrival she was offered the job by the Secretary of the Admiralty. She was told that she had been interviewed without knowing it on a previous occasion.

Starting immediately with her Deputy Director, Angela Goodenough, a "Chief Woman Officer" in the Civil Service at the Admiralty, the two set about creating the new service, making war on traditional stuffiness, working for some time without a secretary, often until eight o'clock at night and taking turns to come in on Saturdays and Sundays. They began to interview and select thousands of applicants, visited the ports to find out what was needed, decided on categories of job, argued over pay and conditions and battled furiously to have the service accepted as part of the Navy instead of coming under Civil Establishments as was thought proper by those in high places. One senior gentleman at the Admiralty said he could see no reason for women wearing uniform, but if they had to "then why should they not all wear khaki?" Ignoring this, and other helpful advice, Vera and her newly joined assistants decided to have a sample uniform made in regular navy serge, known as "Pusser's serge", and took a Wren dressed in it to see Mr. Churchill, then First Lord of the Admiralty. He pronounced the outfit to be "very practical and very dignified". It was unlikely to be changed after that.

As soon as the war began in September of that year, everything accelerated. In a remarkably short time women began to take over hundreds of useful jobs, once considered to be "men's work". As necessity arose, Wrens trained to become radio mechanics, cypher and signal officers, pursers, boats' crews, pay writers, etc. and learnt to handle such jobs as gun inspection, the repair of landing craft and many other categories involving hard physical work and long hours.

As prospective newcomers we were totally unaware of the strength and determination that had been necessary to protect our well-being, but I suspect some concessions had had to be made and drill was possibly one of them. After all, we had to learn to obey instantly - and where for centuries had this been instilled into individuals but on the parade ground? Vera Laughton Matthews herself believed that drill was important and built an esprit-de-corps. To us, at first, it all seemed half-hearted and rather absurd. We thought of it as a bit of a lark.

In those first two weeks we were given a little rudimentary drilling but "dressing by the right" was ludicrous as we were all such different shapes in front, not to mention behind. The Marine Sergeant did his best, roaring and barking like a mad seal. Most of what he bellowed was incomprehensible, but by dint of scampering, looking alert and watching what our neighbours did we somehow shuffled into line, quick marched, halted and stood at ease. I am sure we never got on to anything very advanced. We were probably a complete shambles. We were only there for two weeks and in the Marine Sergeant's opinion a lost cause. He obviously did not feel he could treat us like male recruits and swear at us with volcanic fury and this rather cramped his style.

At the end of the second week we had to face the dreaded tests. It was mainly a question of regurgitating some of the facts we were supposed to have learnt by heart. Most of us got through although two were turned down, we had no idea why.

On the last day we went to be kitted out in rather scratchy serge, uncomfortable black shoes and a souwester type hat with a riband with HMS in gold on it. These hats were later replaced by saucier round caps, like a real sailor's and much preferred by us, but at that time we had to put up with souwesters. The brim in mine flopped too far down, so as soon as I was allowed home on a 48-hour leave I got one of my brothers to thread a wire through the hem of the brim. This strengthened it and I bent it into what I pretended was a becoming curve on the lines of a Romney portrait hat.

I may be wrong but I believe there were only six "set" sizes of uniforms. If you think of the variations of women it can rapidly be understood that some of us looked like refugees, Oliver Twist, or clowns with no hands. The skirt I was given could have housed two. 'If you're as tall as that, the skirt will be as wide as that, sorry.' My mother came to the rescue and narrowed it so that I looked less like a walking lampshade.

The scrubbing? Although this had been part of the traditional training our lot were never asked to show our elbow power. I imagine we may have been among the first groups to undergo probationary training at this extension of Westfield College and I suspect the civilian housekeeper there was not about to let us loose on her floors.

'Have you really been accepted in the Wrens?' One of my brothers was incredulous. 'I suppose they really need people.'

The most exciting part of the Probationary Training Course was learning to salute. The right hand had to come up smartly to the right eye, hand level and flat, thumb hidden, not quite as if you were looking out to sea, but almost. The whole business of saluting made me feel like a principal boy in a pantomime, which was fun, but we were all very nervous at first about who you saluted and when. Out in the streets, actually in uniform, the whole dread business was upon us. However, as you could not get lower than a newly recruited Wren this who-to-salute business was really no problem at all - go for the lot.

The awful plunge was the first time. After getting over this shock it became quite fun learning to spot the amount of gold or blue braid approaching, although I soon realised that we almost ceased to look at faces we were so busy checking sleeves. There was a great deal between the lines of a male-female salute I discovered. It was in fact pregnant with possibilities, as Dornford Yates would have said. There were an infinite number of variations in the acknowledging salute, from mechanical to an interested response. Much later, at a wardroom party on board a destroyer I was told the correct way for a Wren to salute a male officer. Having raised the hand to the eyebrow, one then waggled the fingers up and down, at the same time emitting an Indian war cry. I never tried out this interesting variation.

Now I had to get myself to Greenwich for the two week teleprinter course. It would seem idiotically simple to go from Golders Green station to Greenwich with one small suitcase but for me it felt like going to one of the Poles. I planned the journey carefully with my father, checking where I had to make the changes. I had a free pass, with the statement that I was "proceeding on duty", a stately phrase.

The first surprise was the difference my uniform made. It was quite amazing: I had walked into a world of friendly acceptance. In the train everyone talked to me, not only civilians who wanted to know where I was off to - we had been told to parry this sort of question on the enemy-is-everywhere theory - but everyone in every sort of uniform took me for a mate. We were fellow sufferers, we all had shoes that pinched, our uniforms were hot, we were in a bloody awful situation taking orders from everybody, but we all shared in this predicament, thanks to bloody Hitler. It was suddenly tremendously exhilarating. Between Waterloo and New Cross I was offered four cigarettes, ate someone's extra bun and looked appreciatively at squashed photographs of girl-friends, wives and children. I suppose I guessed my own place in the class line-up but I suddenly knew that the days of silly snobbery were dead. Those awesome instructions while growing up - what *one* does or does not do - could, within reason, go out of the window. In the train, I was packed in among friendly faces and strongly smelling uniforms and I felt I had got my ticket to life. I was part of the wartime scene instead of distant from it as I had been in civilian clothes. All of us in uniform shared an incognito. We were all still us inside the khaki, light and dark blue serge but we need not necessarily play the old role, we could try out another persona - no-one would know. It was also like joining a shoal of herring, all we had to do was swim and veer with the rest.

As Wrens, we were highly regarded herrings I discovered. People queueing for a bus to Greenwich pushed another Wren and myself to the front of the queue and the conductor pulled our legs and said if we were ever in the Red Lion, I forget where, he would stand us a drink.

The bus dropped us a few yards from the Palace of Greenwich. It was a sparkling sunlit morning. In front of us was the great river and there upon it were all manner of ships. Like Pepys before me, on much the same spot, I smelt a waft of sea tang and heard the clopping of water against boats at anchor, the slap of ropes and flap of sails in the stiff breeze. To everything connected to the sea I became more than ever committed.

Behind us was the "Queen's House" built for Anne of Denmark and finished for Henrietta Maria, with its unbroken view of the river between the two arms of the Palace. The sound of doves cooing echoed round the centre square. There was a sense of order, cleanliness and discipline; men and women in uniforms, which were better fitting than mine, crossed up and down and when meeting directly saluted each other. We managed a salute or two ourselves without falling over backwards or knocking our hats off. We reported to the Wren Officer in charge. I felt like Alice after the "Eat Me" magic.

The teleprinter course was frustrating. It disliked the pressure I was used to from pounding my old typewriter. I tamed it by realising that you had to caress the keys instead of hitting them and then it stopped jamming up angrily, making a noise like fifty imprisoned hornets.

The electronic magic of being able to type a message in one place and it being instantaneously received in the place you were calling seemed too amazing to try to understand. We were told on pain of all sorts of dire consequences that we must never waste precious lines on "chat". As it happened, the Naval Base I was sent to had only one machine which was attached to the main office across a river. On night duty we did occasionally break this rule - no other lines could be held up: 'U all rt?' 'Fine, how R U?' and other unenthralling but friendly exchanges. The fact that we never met the person on duty at the other end somehow added to the miraculous business. There was a "call button" which when you pressed it made the machine go crazy for a few seconds while it tapped out the call sign of the machine you were connected to. The difficult part was knowing the way to route your message and who was connected to whom. This was a complicated business of calling up the main switching stations and asking to be put through. A funny sounding place called Cambuslang was one of the big stations, obviously part of a Jabberwocky world.

Sharing a room with another lot of strangers was a bore. Most of us were shy of dressing and undressing in front of others, only a few dashing spirits seemed not to care. I used to get up early and having paced out the territory, found a bathroom that seemed out on a limb.   Here I had a quick bath every morning and dressed in private, risking getting into trouble as we had been told we could only have a bath every three days.   I excused myself to myself by using the minimum amount of water.   The skill was evading the others.   No-one else found my secret bathroom.   The bath was huge and very corroded and had a plug handle in a separate column outside the bath.   It was foolish but an exciting exercise in nonconformity.

At the end of the course we were to be "posted" to a Naval or Fleet Air Arm base.   The choice of verb made me feel like a parcel, but the worrying part was exactly where we would end up.   It was not a particularly pleasant thought that our fate was so entirely at the whim of someone else.   With his experience of the army, my father had warned that if I wanted somewhere in the south I should ask for Scapa Flow.   I thought it best to say nothing and hope.

6.

I had secretly favoured Portsmouth . . . I got Hull.

"From Hell, Hull and Halifax, good Lord protect us." We were gleefully informed of this by a native soon after arrival.

All the family came to see me off from King's Cross, which was a bit throat tightening, but as soon as the train pulled out and started its rhythmical swaying and chuntering through the English countryside I felt elated. Trains are soothing. You can't get out when you feel like it so you might as well sit back and enjoy the scenery. A certain calm of inevitability came upon me. It *was* after all, for me, a great adventure.

On arrival at Hull Station a complete stranger offered us a cup of tea in the Station Canteen. There were three of us and we had met up on Doncaster Station where we had to change for Hull. We were Fox, Flux and Mack. The music hall combination of our three names, we learnt, had caused the Naval Base personnel much laughter when the signal announcing our arrival was received. Fox was a roly-poly girl, black hair and red cheeks and merry; Flux was angular and serious.

That Station Canteen was amazing. The air was so thick from smoke and fug that it was hard to see anyone. It was always crowded and was used by Forces personnel as their home from home. The tea was strong enough to stand on, and we drank it out of chipped, thick-rimmed cups which had suffered from many savage washings-up. There were also eggless, butterless, tasteless cakes that were like momentos of the Sahara. But the atmosphere of jolly camaraderie was wonderful, chiefly engendered by the canteen staff, humorous and friendly. We soon got to know them all by name and had to stand up to being teased in broad Yorkshire. An exclamation, much used was "Eee, what a bugger", even for unexceptional acts like forgetting to put sugar into someone's tea. When I later used this expression, which had become absolutely part of my vocabulary, my father restrained me. 'Do you know what a "bugger" is?' I didn't. He didn't explain but asked me not to use it at home.

Hull had suffered very severely in the blitz. From the station we immediately saw the damaged buildings and the heaps of rubble.   The Royal Station Hotel stood four square but there seemed to be very few complete buildings around it.   The Wrenery was Number Four, West Parade, Anlaby Road, not far from the station, but there was no room for us there and we three newcomers were assigned to families.   Fox and Flux stayed together and I was sent down a long, suburban road to stay with a delightful lady whose son was a pilot in the Fleet Air Arm.   These households were informed that they would have to put someone up, with no choice either way.   With luck, I got a real Yorkshire welcome from a very lovable person.   I stayed with her for a few weeks before there was room for me at the Wrenery. I continued to write to Mrs. Blanchard for several years.   When the handsome son, Alan, in the photograph on the mantelpiece, arrived home on leave he brought Mrs. Blanchard kirby grips and dozens of pairs of silk stockings, and face cream for his girl friend in the WAAF.   I hope he survived and gave Mrs. B. lots of grandchildren.

Hull Naval Base was a bit of a disappointment.   It was nothing grander than a number of terraced houses made intercommunicating.   Our "Signal Distribution Office" was obviously the back kitchen and scullery of one of them.   The teleprinter, a single machine, was in what must have been the larder. The place was not inspiring, rather damp and smelling of mildew and of old roast dinners which had somehow seeped into the walls.   None of this seemed to matter; the pleasures, or the reverse, of being "on watch" depended entirely on who was on duty with you.   There were usually four of us, with a Leading Wren in charge, and despite the amount of work, we joked and laughed and play-acted and generally got up to any larks that were possible.   One of our delights was to send out for fish and chips, which arrived hot and greasy in old newspaper.   It tasted wonderful. Work had to continue as we ate and we occasionally had to discard the copy of a signal with a large tell-tale greasy fingerprint on it and roll off another copy.   Using the copying machine made our fingers purple and the fish and chip paper sometimes looked as if it had contained squids.

The four Leading Wrens in charge of each Watch were "Immobile", a category meaning that for family reasons they had joined up on the condition that they could not be sent anywhere else. All four lived in the area around Hull. In the first watch I joined I was made to understand that I was exceedingly lucky, as their watch was undoubtedly the best, with the nicest Leading Wren in charge. There seemed to be a bit of "House" rivalry. Their great butt of dislike was an older woman, Leading Wren of the watch which took over from ours. They hated her chiefly, I discovered, because of her determination to be comfortable on night watch. We were supposed to be alert and ready to deal with any material which came in over night, but very often there was not very much and you could get as comfortable as an upright chair would allow and drop off to sleep with your head on the desk. This was not good enough for Miss Woodhouse. I was told that she made a leading seaman on night duty set up a folding bed for her - which they said was a scandalous misuse of her authority. I gathered that she also had a sharp tongue and had criticised their distribution of the signals which had come in. This distribution was the job of the Leading Wren of the Watch who had to decide which members of the various heads of department should have a copy of each signal; this was a vital task, requiring a good knowledge of the function of each department. There was a duty officer who could be consulted but it was a point of honour not to disturb him, particularly at night, unless a really important or knotty problem signal was received.

After some time I was suddenly told that I was to move to Woody's Watch - Woody the dragon. This was a blow. No more anecdotes and jokes; Woody's team were serious-minded. From what they cheerfully told me I was in for a rough time with the autocratic and comfort-loving Miss Woodhouse.

The lowest of the low, ie: the newest person to join a watch, does any dogsbodying going and all the jobs that nobody else likes doing. This included making the tea. This in fact was a nice thing to do. It took you off the routine job of sitting at a typewriter or teleprinter, enabled you to move around, boil a funny battered kettle on a stove, go in search of milk and biscuits and breathe fresh air. I enjoyed trying to remember who liked what and setting the steaming mugs in front of everyone. It was nice and domestic and the heirarchy involved seemed pointless.

"Woody" was a lady in her early thirties, certainly older than any of the other Wrens I had worked with. She considered herself a lady, with all the connotations of those days. She was also, as I discovered in due course, an eccentric. She had a very sharp manner, which I could see terrified her subordinates. She did not take kindly to sloppy or slow work. There was a tension among her team, no idle chatter to enliven the duty hours; it was all a very serious business.

Woody ordered me to make her tea and gave careful instructions: 'Weak, mind you. I like it weak. Don't bring me any of that burnt sienna stuff'. I duly made all the five teas, carefully sloshing a gallon of hot water into Woody's cup (she provided her own cup and saucer, had it washed up and then locked up when she went off duty, along with her private folding bed, pillow and two rugs). I cannot remember why I was suddenly so emboldened, or so cheeky, but I put Woody's cup in front of her saying loudly and cheerfully 'Weak tea for the weak'. There was a stunned silence. All the other members of her watch gasped or stared, while I popped round the hot mugs of strong stand-up tea for everyone else. Suddenly Woody laughed. 'You've made it just as I like it,' she said.

I had got under a net. After this curious remark we never looked back. Having found that I could make Woody laugh, I built on this and we began to take each other's measure. I respected her wish for comfort on night watch and only wished I had my own folding bed. Maddening as she often was, she started, very unselfishly and skilfully, to teach me everything she knew about being head of a watch so that in time I knew the work well enough to become head of a watch myself.

But there was danger in being Woody's acolyte. A week or two after joining her watch I got a telephone call at the Wrenery. The telephone was in a confined position under the stairs and the ear piece, as usual, had been left hanging on the chord. I picked it up. It was the Leading Wren "friend" from my old watch.

'You needn't think you're going to get anywhere with Miss Woodhouse,' a harsh voice said. She almost spat down the telephone. 'You must ask to come off her watch at once or we shall go to her and tell her what you've said about her.'

I can remember being more astounded by this than by anything that had happened to me before. I looked at the earpiece of the phone as people do in films, unbelieving. What *was* she talking about? Was this the girl I had thought so friendly? This was blackmail. She and her watch must have been told that I was getting on with Woody. Where was the harm in that? What struck me as almost comical was that while I had joined in the fun and the laughs at Woody's expense it was they who had gossiped about her, it was their game. If they went to Woody with nasty tales, I had a few I could tell. It was an important moment for I was entirely shocked by this volte face. This was evil. I pulled myself together and told her to do exactly as she pleased and go to the devil and I crashed the phone back on its hook. I had to lean against the wall with shock. How had I so misjudged that girl? What motivated her? The war between watches and I had crossed over to the enemy? Or did she foresee that being a Mobile Wren, I should gain from Woody's guidance and be put forward for a commission?

One of our "relaxations" turned out to be more demanding than fun. These were dances arranged in drill halls. They were always packed to the doors with what were rather snobbily called "other ranks", with three times as many men as women. There was little ventilation, owing to the stringencies of the blackout and everyone was a smoker. The stuffiness, lack of air and exuberance ensured that soon perspiration flowed and we seemed to drown in the overpowering smell of soaked serge. The trouble was that as Wrens we were the sailors' choice, which should have been delightful except that, as dancers, they were too good. Apparently a lot of ratings whiled away the long voyages dancing with each other and perfecting the latest steps. This meant that as soon as we arrived we were whirled straight into one energetic foxtrot after another, one's partner expecting expertise with all the twinkling quick-quick-slow, lock-in-and-out steps or, as the music changed, suddenly and exaggeratingly held by a strong left arm and propelled in the small of one's back with an equally strong right in a vigorous, back-bending swirl of a tango.   Facing it squarely I knew I would never reach their standard.   Ginger Rogers I was not.

An odd thing was that as a beanpole it was *always* the shortest matelot who asked me to dance first.   Gazing down on curly tops or sleek hair-oiled heads, I strove to follow, their noses about level with my tummy button, my feet in flat-heeled shoes going faster and faster and usually out of my control.   I liked the mickey-taking ones best who expertly mimicked my too southern accent: 'I say, not quite the Savoy, what?'   To which the best reply was 'Oh, I prefer this, the floor's too small at the Savoy.'

7

Hull docks were our raison d'être, vital busy areas full of the sound of iron striking hollow metal, the affront of a drill, a clanking of machines and trucks, shuntings and revings, shouts of the dock workers, acetylene flares, and creaking grinding cranes. There were reminders of the long trade links with the East in a street name: "The Land of Green Ginger" and, most exciting of all were the ships of light or dark grey, top heavy with guns and weird-looking bits of strange equipment.

The majority of the ships coming in for repairs and refits were destroyers and corvettes, many of which had been badly damaged in enemy action. We knew from the signals which ships were arriving and as soon as they docked a telephone was connected. Very often the first calls came through to us in the Signal Distribution Office to check if there were any important messages for them. We soon appreciated that we were often the first woman the caller had spoken to for months and it was sometimes quite a flirtatious affair, much frowned on by Woody if we went on chatting for too long.

As the ship was being tied up to her appointed dock, the most eagerly awaited item on board was the Mail Bag of letters for the ship's company. The Wren in charge of the Mail Room made it a point of honour to get the post to the ship as soon as she docked, knowing how desperately the men were waiting for news of their wives, families and girl friends. As soon as the formalities were gone through, most of the officers and men went on leave, leaving a skeleton crew on board. A fleet of cars, with Wren drivers, arrived at the dock to take those going on leave to the station.

The Hull Wren drivers were the crème-de-la-crème. They were easily the most attractive girls in the Wrenery and three of them were in my "cabin" of eight, known as HMS Vivacious. We had been adopted by a destroyer of that name and the ship's handsome crest painted in gold on wood, hung over the mantelpiece. It was an apt name as the drivers particularly were a marvellous lively funny group. Apart from the odd invitation via the Signal Office these girls had the parties on board ship sewn up. The skeleton staff left on board had to have some amusement and who best to organise this than the pretty merry drivers whose cars, for duty visits, were at their disposal. The leading lights in party organisation were Anne, a bouncy, big-busted girl of immense energy and a cracking sense of humour and devilry, and Joan, her great friend, a very pretty girl with little puff curls at each side of her cheeks like a French marquise. Eileen was short and slim with a translucent best-china complexion. These three had some amazing tales of driving an Admiral or Captain through the night: they had no proper headlights as they had to be blacked out except for a small hole, and all the signposts had been removed so as not to assist an invader. They had stories of being invited to such and such a party, of flirtations and nascent love affairs until the rest of us often had to beg them to shut up so that we could get some sleep. Their friendship had been welded and tested in the heavy raids and they had some breathtaking escape stories to tell. From the length of time they had been driving for Hull Naval Base they had a network of contacts. So wide had the net spread that it was not unusual for a newly docked ship to ask for "Joan", "Anne" or "Eileen" on arrival. The word had got round.

A wardroom party on board one of His Majesty's destroyers was the "Palace" invitation of our existence. We had to apply for a late pass, and even then we were supposed to be back in the Wrenery by eleven thirty. Very often the outer door had been shut and we had to be hoisted and shoved into a ground floor cabin which luckily had a window on to the street. It was high off the ground and the pushing and shoving was quite an effort for our attendant cavaliers or the helpful taxi driver.

Getting ready for the party was a hilarious business in itself. Very few had been able to find, or afford, the black silk stockings which were so preferable to the opaque issue variety, but for those of the same size these precious silk ones were almost held in common. Whoever had a spare pair lent them for the occasion and had a return match next time. There never seemed to be any hassle over this, it was assumed that anyone with the luck to have an invitation had first call on the stockings. Apart from this, "dressing" consisted of a clean white shirt, highly polished shoes and, of course, make-up. This would also seem a simple affair but it was not. Very little make-up of any sort was available. Yardleys and Cyclax existed but were hard to find. Occasionally a consignment of American make-up got through the blockade - Max Factor, Elizabeth Arden or Harriet Hubbard Ayer. To find this you had to be persistent and lucky.

In Hull, the splendid store, Thornton and Varley, was our Souk. It was full of whatever Utility garments one might wish to imagine oneself wearing as a civilian and the occasional allocations of cosmetics. Actually finding an item that we liked, such as a particular shade and make of lipstick, was like trying to track down a Swallowtail butterfly. Going shopping was altogether like going on safari: we never quite knew if today we should bag a lion or a lizard or no meat at all. The system of doling out supplies when they came in was strict but we certainly benefited from extreme kindness on the part of the employees behind the counter. We would pass by for a casual chat whenever we were in the shop. If no other customers were breathing down our necks, our benefactress would glance quickly to right and left and reach below the counter, handing over a wrapped package saying merely 'Five and eleven three', or whatever the price was. If we had any money at all, which wasn't often, we would smile and thank, pay and hurry away to see what we had got from the Bran Tub. If we were skint, there was a hurried movement of re-concealment and out of the corner of her mouth the assistant would hiss 'Keep it for you for next week'. How wonderfully they raised our morale. I hope we expressed our gratitude properly for such undoubted favouritism.

Once ready we would share a taxi to whichever dock "our" ship was in. At the Dockyard Gate we had to be passed in by the Sergeant-at-Arms who had been given our names. The taxi then manoeuvred round intricate narrow ways in the dark to find our particular ship. It was very very dark, since lights could not be shown in Black Out, but there in the twilight lay the ship, tethered with several umbilical cords to the dock side, a lovely graceful object of grey metal. Sometimes the ship lay shining in the moonlight, a worrying time as she would show up too clearly if there happened to be an air raid. Sometimes the smell of the

34

docks was astonishing; the Fish Dock in particular hit you with an olfactory assault that almost took your nose off, but somehow, once on board, the smell partially disappeared or we got used to it, or forgot it in the excitement. We would be welcomed on board and taken to one of the officer's cabins to comb our hair, blown all over the place by the wind coming in across the Humber river. One or two of us carried earrings in our pockets to cheer up the occasion and this was the moment we put them on.

We were then escorted to the Wardroom. This seemed very small for the full complement of the ship's officers to live and work in at sea. Even though the engine, the ship's heartbeat, was silent, there always seemed to be the hum of a generator somewhere. Each ship had its own special personality and there was an extra pride in destroyers, these "maids of all work" as they were called; small but dangerous, they were not to be trifled with. I felt the spirit of Drake was in the very rivets.

Some wardrooms felt happier than others, with a feeling of friendly cheer and camaraderie; some had a more formal atmosphere, depending entirely on the personality of the officers. So much hung on the character of the commanding officer, and whether he, or a senior member of the wardroom, was present. The liveliest evenings tended to be when the junior members were on their own.

Every wardroom was presided over by the portraits of the King and Queen, and when it came to the loyal toast, we raised our glasses in their direction. By naval tradition, the loyal toast was drunk seated, a practical necessity owing to the smallness of the wardroom and the height of some of the officers.

Dinners on board were splendid affairs, with white napery, wine glasses, fine decanters and good food, served by the wardroom stewards with flair. Occasionally there was something exotic brought back from overseas and once we were given bananas. Bananas! We had not seen a banana since the beginning of war. A glass of precious orange juice, brought from the States, seemed like a goblet of golden nectar. This was all in joyous contrast to our scrubbed tables and tin spoons at the

Wrenery, not to mention the eternal spam and reconstituted potato.

Just occasionally, in the middle of the jollification, there came a moment of wondering what it must be like to be shut up in that wardroom on patrol somewhere. We knew that such and such a ship had "seen enemy action" and had limped home, its company nursing their wounded and mourning their dead. Nothing of this was ever referred to unless the story had some humorous content or absurdity - it was not a suitable subject for a party, and anyway such things were best forgotten *if* you could temporarily forget them. Also no facts, events or places, were ever mentioned; careless talk cost lives.

It was in 1940 that Grand Admiral Doenitz had boasted "I will show that the U-boat alone can win this war. Nothing is impossible to us." Germany had fifty-seven operational U-boats at the outbreak of war; they were the corps d'élite of the German Navy and by 1942 the huge building yards available to Germany, including French and Dutch yards, had turned out three hundred and four U-boats. The Atlantic was the vital supply line which they concentrated on breaking - all the more important now that American troups and supplies were coming east. The U-boats, controlled from Germany, operated everywhere, searching for weak spots in our defences, sinking the merchant ships at an average of forty a month. Germany, too, by 1942, possessed operational bases from North Cape to the French border with Spain, and when Italy came into the war the U-boats were reinforced by one hundred Italian submarines.

Against this formidable threat the Convoy System had been brought into operation almost as soon as war broke out, using the experience of the First World War when the convoys had not been started until quite late (May 1917). The leading role in the protection of the convoys were the destroyers and corvettes. We were as convinced as the ship's company that they were part of our lifeline to victory. We shared the conviction that to command the seas was our natural heritage. Hitler had challenged our supremacy, he would have to be shown a thing or two.

Every ship, of course a "she", was a temperamental lady with her own tricks and foibles and her ship's company were proud of her, anxiously watching over her repairs, exhorting the invading work force to take particular care of her. On most evenings our hosts luckily assumed we would like to see over their ship. We would exclaim at the ingenious use of space. Most of the officers' cabins were so small they were more like cupboards; as for the men's quarters it seemed almost unbelievable that the ship could accommodate so many in such cramped conditions. I wondered how the lack of space and the smell of oil and metal would seem if you felt seasick. In the galleys the shining metal pots and pans and the white-robed figures mixing vaporous concoctions was reminiscent of Macbeth's witches, of the opposite sex. It was like a royal visit for we were mightily stared at. Amidst the steam and bubbling it seemed required procedure to make the sort of silly remark that visiting VIPs attempt such as "Umm, that looks good", meaning the last thing you want to do is taste the brew. The easiest way was just to exchange grins. Clattering up and down the companion ways, or ladders, I tried to concentrate on not showing too much of my bloomers and trying not to imagine what one would feel like if one of the steel bulkheads suddenly buckled like tinfoil under the impact of a torpedo.

Fear, of course, was never talked about; it was too great a problem for all but the most insouciant. 1942 was the worst year for destroyer losses when forty-six ships were sunk. The total losses for the war were one hundred and thirty-nine destroyers and twenty-eight corvettes.

8

Working night watches was a bore. Akin to jet lag, which we knew nothing about in 1942, the body timing resents being turned upside down. I used to get stomach ache and found it hard to sleep in the day, especially as the other inmates of HMS Vivacious were drivers and secretaries who would pop into the cabin from time to time, kindly going on tiptoe but this, in heavy black shoes on an uncarpeted floor did not make an appreciable difference. I should have hated to share with other "watch keepers" however. I was extremely happy where I was. My bunk mate was another Joan, a small dainty girl to whom I ceded the top bunk - if the Wrenery got a direct hit and she had fallen on me, no problem, if I had collapsed on top of her it might have been disastrous.

The good thing was being free in the daytime, plenty of time to haunt the shops, including one called Carmichaels, which drew us like a magnet. Carmichaels had two display windows, which because they were inside a heavy metal outside shutter could be left free of boarding, or strips of criss-crossed paper to prevent flying glass. It was owned, I believe, by Ian Carmichael's parents and was a treasure house of elegant objects meant to be given as wedding, anniversary, birthday or Christmas gifts. There were a few pretty objects which were within our modest range, although most of the time we gazed like one of Dickens' children at the glass, china and table silver lying in red velvet boxes. We got a lot of pleasure remembering that beautiful objects could still be bought. Just occasionally we had enough cheek to go in and ask a price; very rarely did we actually buy anything.

Friends were vital: someone to meet and have coffee with in the Georgian tea rooms, or the rather grand Station Hotel, someone to moan to about problems and go shopping with. We needed friends since we were separated from everything previously known, and while we talked interminably about our families and aired our egos, some very good friendships developed. There was an attractive girl in the next-door cabin, also a driver, called Eira. Animated and restless, her blonde hair, quite long, had to be rolled up neatly on duty, but off duty it flew out behind her in the wind. We were not supposed to allow our hair to reach our collars. Going out with her was a zigzag business as she had to touch every pillar box we passed to make superstitiously sure of the arrival of letters from her husband serving overseas. Another great friend was Mary, very humorous and sweet-natured, a novelist's ideal heroine, also tall, blonde and blue-eyed. She was a Christian Scientist, which meant that we had some strong arguments. She was a talented pianist. She tackled the upright piano at the Wrenery as if it were a Steinway. The Warsaw Concerto was our favourite, particularly if we were down in the dumps.

Hull's theatre was a great source of excitement. There were plays and concerts and once or twice the stage door keeper let me in behind the scenes to sit on a laundry basket and hear a concert for nothing.

This sort of particular kindness to those in uniform we met with everywhere. When I telephoned home, which I did once a week from under the stairs, I would assemble the necessary coins and ring the operator - no dialing direct in those days. Several times whoever was on duty would open a conversation: 'Hello, how are we?' 'Fine, thanks, and you?' 'Can't complain. Are you phoning home?' 'Yes, I am.' 'Go ahead. No charge.'

A surprising request came through to the Wrenery. A Mr. Harbottle requested the loan of three tall Wrens. A production of "Merrie England" by the unfortunately named Edward German was to be put on. The local Choral Society had been asked to provide singers and extras; the stars would be coming from London and were well-known professional singers.

Three of us volunteered; we were the obvious choice anyway since no-one else came up to our ears. It was an extremely welcome break in routine. We went along to a church hall for rehearsals and found we were required to be heralds; three very handsome costumes arrived in due course, elaborate, gold-embroidered, supposedly copies of a sixteenth-century herald's attire. We were told to take great care of them as they were worth two hundred pounds each.

As heralds we would be keeping our mouths shut until the moment came to pretend to blow a fanfare, but luckily there was also a place for us in two other scenes as part of the crowd. This meant that we were included in the choral rehearsals. The music was easy for beginners, very catchy tunes and stirringly patriotic. It was exactly the right show for wartime and had already been successfully put on in other parts of the country by the same company using local talent. The leading singers were due to arrive for final rehearsals and in the meantime we met two or three times a week to learn the music and the crowd movements.

Rehearsals in the rather ill-lit hall were fun and quite moving. Most of the male choir were firemen, civil defence volunteers or policemen. They came to rehearsal in uniform, hanging up their tin hats or helmets on the schoolroom hooks along one wall. One of the great songs from the score is the Yeoman of England, powerful patriotic stuff. There were six firemen and two policemen who sang the song, with fine strong voices, defending Elizabeth I's England. It was exactly what they were doing for George VI three hundred and fifty years later. In the dress rehearsal it was splendid to see them at last in costume but for me the song had total heart-stopping power when they sang it in their wartime service clothes holding imaginery bows and dropping on one knee on the wooden floor.

One afternoon I was waiting to cross a main street in the middle of Hull, thoughts miles away, when I realised the policeman on point duty had held up all the traffic for me. As I crossed to the centre island I heard a broad Yorkshire voice say 'See you at the rehearsal.' It was our leading bowman. He told Eira later that evening that she had almost run over his toes when he signalled her line of traffic to move.

As soon as the principals arrived the tensions and excitement grew. We went backstage to find the dressingroom assigned to us and were instructed in our make-up. The smell of the greasepaint lived up to its famous magic. For years afterwards I had only to catch a whiff of its sour-sweet powdery smell to recapture the heady thrill of the truly stagestruck.

Queen Elizabeth was sung by a woman with a powerful contralto and a fine presence. I have forgotten her name, but she was overpoweringly queenlike in red wig, golden robes and a ruff like an enlarged halo. When she came to the front of the stage to sing her best song "Sword and buckler by thy side, rest on the shores of battle-tide, which like the ever-hungry sea, howls round this isle . . . Oh slee-eep, till I awaken thee, and in they slumber, smile," the audience went wild with delight and roared for an encore.

The tenor who had the part of the Earl of Essex was extremely good-looking on stage, with reddish brown wig and beard, and all the Wrens who came to see the play fell in love with him and begged us for his autograph. For us, who had seen him off-key and sometimes bad-tempered, the attraction was not quite so potent. But the power of the theatre is strong, for despite what we thought of him off stage when he was in full court attire to attend the Queen it was very easy to share the infatuation of our friends. After being heralds, holding our golden trumpets silently while the brass in the orchestra blew our notes, we had to rush off to change and fling on peasant costumes of artistic chiffon rags. There was very little time before we had to dash below the stage and along a narrow corridor to enter for the next scene on the prompt side. On one occasion he stopped in the corridor as we approached and bowed elaborately with a sweep of his velvet cap. We responded with deep curtseys. Time had evaporated. For just three seconds we caught an impression of Tudor England, almost as if we had been privileged to curtsey to the great Essex himself. It was a trick of the dim light and the magic of Edward German's splendid score.

Joan, my upper bunk partner, had a ticket for one of the performances towards the end of the week. I had told her to come round and see us in our dressing-room in the main interval and she duly appeared. One of our peasants was away sick that evening and her dress lay over the back of a chair. In that instant an idea occurred to me. The girl was small, about the same size as Joan. I told her to put the costume on and join us on the stage. She was horrified but we persuaded her at least to try it on. Then we told her just to follow us in the crowd scene, look as if she were singing and do whatever we did. We made her up rapidly: we had bare feet so shoes were no problem. Almost before she was ready, there was the bell to end the interval and the thrilling fearful cry of the callboy 'On stage, ladies and gentlemen'. We danced on in our trippingly Maypole manner, Joan obediently following, then we bunched to one side to sing the chorus of the next big number.

Joan had been sitting with two friends in the stalls and when she did not return they were anxious. 'What has happened to her? Do you think one of us should go and see?' 'No, she'll be back in a moment. She's probably been in a queue for the loo.' When Joan rejoined them at the next interval they wouldn't believe that she had been on stage.

The senior Wren in charge of us all was First Officer Nancy Williams, very approachable, a warm-hearted lady. She was in the middle of a battle with the officer in charge of Communications, a stubborn Yorkshireman and a Lieutenant, a lower rank than her own but supported, she suspected, by the Captain of the Base. She had been told by Wren Headquarters to put forward the names of anyone who might be suitable to hold a commission. When she did so, the Lieutenant, and one or two other higher ranks in charge of departments, refused to authorise her recommendations. 'We've just got the Wrens trained to do the work properly and I won't have you taking them away,' was the Lieutenant's line, practical perhaps from his point of view but shortsighted. What a brute, we thought, that means we shall be here for life. Until we were told about this, the thought had not occurred that any of us might be officer material, we had just assumed that Hull was our job for the period of the war. This injected a dose of ambition into some of us. The opportunity to advance in our Wren careers ought not to be thwarted by men who only thought of their own convenience. This was really old-fashioned, but it looked as if they held all the cards.

After a big fight she got my friend, Mary, to attend a Board in London where she was accepted for the Officers' Training Course at Greenwich. In no time at all, it seemed, Mary had written and sent a photograph of herself in the elegant uniform

42

and beautiful tricorne hat.   It was a precedent but the Lieutenant didn't think so.

But our First Officer was a determined character.   She could also scare us rigid.   Nancy Williams owned a baby Austin.   She was generous in giving lifts if we were ever on our way into the middle of town from the Base.   She had to park carefully because, as she confessed one day with a rueful smile, 'I've never learnt to reverse.'   It was a hair-raising business being driven by her.   If one was in the back seat she would turn almost completely round to talk, seeming to forget that she was at the wheel.

'Mack, I've put your name forward for a commission,' she said one afternoon when she was giving a lift to three of us.

'Oh, thank you very much, Mam.'

'We'll beat Lieutenant X.   I just will *not* allow him to stop any more of my recommendations.'   She wrenched the car round a corner, turning round to see my reaction, regardless of pedestrians, dogs, others cars and a traffic policeman.   I had my mouth open ready to shout "Look Out!" and thought that if I managed to survive this car journey the idea was delightful. That evening I realised there was another problem, before aiming for that enviable velvety tricorne one had first to get through the Board.

9

At the Wrenery we had to sign a book if we intended to spend the night away, stating where we were going.   Scatterbrain Mack had already got into serious trouble by forgetting to sign out on two occasions.   I had met a couple in the theatre, a doctor and his wife, whom I had sat next to in the stalls and they had invited me several times when I was off duty to stay with them. The Wren officer in charge of the Wrenery was fierce, she was a headmistress personified and she warned me of awesome consequences if I forgot again.   Now I can sympathise with her weighty responsibilities but then I just regarded her as an old fuss-pot - she must have been all of twenty-six.

A missive arrived telling me to report to Queen Anne's Mansions in London at 2.30 on a Tuesday.   To get there in time it was necessary to catch an early train from Hull.   In the train, dressed in my well-brushed best uniform, well-polished shoes and discreet make-up, I remember suddenly sitting up in the carriage like a mechanical pin at a bowling alley . . . I had forgotten to sign that wretched book in the hall.

Such a small thing but now, even if I passed the dreaded Board, this was the end.   The officer in charge of us would not see any humour in the situation and would certainly put in a bad report over unofficer-like behaviour.   How could one be relied upon in a position of responsibility if one couldn't remember the simplest routine etc . . . all was lost.   It was pointless to continue to London at the Nation's expense;   I must catch the next train back to Hull and ignominy.   I would change at Doncaster.

DONCASTER.   I had to change there anyway for the London train.   There was at least fifteen minutes to wait and there was, I remembered, a telephone box on the platform.   I rushed to the telephone, got through to bunk-mate Joan and asked her to sign me out.   Getting someone else to write your name in the book was luckily not a crime - the point was for the Wrenery to have a record of where we all were.   SALVATION.

Joan was amused that I had forgotten, took it all calmly and promised to save my life immediately.   As I left the telephone booth and the train for London rumbled in, hissing at us impatiently, my elation rate reached boiling point.   Doors were slamming, the whistle blew, we were off.   It was difficult not to burst into a rendering of "Sword and Buckler" but, finding a window seat I managed to open a book and stare at the scene outside without seeing the words or the countryside.   It was like a bang on the head;   all my self doubts about my suitability to be an officer, which had really been confirmed by carelessness, disappeared.   I suddenly thought I *could* take responsibility, concentrate on what mattered and cease mucking about.   I was reminded of Woody's dictum: 'check your signal distribution, double check, then check again; third and fourth thoughts are better than leaving someone out.   Refuse to be hurried. Accuracy is all.'

On arrival in London I had about an hour to spare.   Having eaten some awful sandwiches at King's Cross I decided on a morale booster.   I went to find the loo at Claridges.   I had been in this particular haven once or twice before.   The older lady who presided like an empress over the gleaming hand-basins was an artist: she would hand a clean towel at the precise moment you needed one, had a good strong brush to de-dandruff collars, handed out pins and new kirby grips, had been known to mend a tear in a garment and fix a broken heel and goodness knew what besides.   She had plenty of stories of a rather hair-raising nature of narrow squeaks from incendiaries and high explosive bombs. She was always cheerful.   There came a moment when she would just shift the little china dish for tips a centimetre while continuing to talk, almost as if it had moved out of place of its own accord.   There were always a few coins laid in the dish 'pour encourager les autres'.

The softened lights, the elegance, the smell of expensive perfume, even in those wartime deprived days, made one recollect a safe world where war did not exist and it gave the edge to my confidence.   I caught a bus to Hyde Park Corner and walked across St. James's Park, stopping on the bridge to look at the ducks.   There were a number of interesting ministerial types walking about, bowler-hatted and talking earnestly, as well as a number of Navy, Army and Air Force brass hats, whom I had to salute. The little park seemed cared for, despite the war, and full of vital people directing affairs and pursuing the war. It was the very hub of the great wheel.

On to Queen Anne's Mansions and back to nervous twitching, which took over fast as I joined a roomful of other nervous-looking Wrens. At intervals a name was called. It seemed a long business. As at my first interview in this building, the interviewees did not reappear. Was this so that we should not meet and get useful information? What would we be asked? Supposing there was a question that I couldn't answer? Bluff or 'I'm sorry I don't know?' I heard my name called.

It was a smaller room than I expected, with a table behind which sat, not just women as I had imagined but a naval Captain with four resplendent gold rings, and three Wren officers. Vera Laughton Matthews, known by us affectionately as Tugboat Annie, was not there. I don't know why I thought she would be. Presiding was an attractive slender lady - Lady Cholmondely I later discovered. She was giving out a cheerful aura of don't-worry-about-this-too-much, take-it-in-your-stride, which got across to me as I walked to a chair, placed ominously and prisoner-at-the-bar fashion in front of their eminences.

The Captain had an eyeglass which reminded me of a joke of my father's about a Colonel who could throw up his monocle and catch it in his eye. I waited for this monocle to fall at some reply of mine. They all asked questions in turn, some in a kind tone, others crisply and in no-nonsense fashion. I answered as best I could. I was still breathing. Of course I don't remember a single question, but I do remember being encouraged to talk about a job I had done for a friend of my father's, which consisted of assembling ships' models for the Admiralty Inspector and subsequently posting them to training establishments for aircraft recognition. A pleasant thought is that there is no video of that interview and I don't have to sit through it again. But I was in. That soft, mole-velvet black tricorne with its handsome blue and gold insignia was to be mine after all.

Back in Hull, waiting the call to attend the Officers' Training Course, we had an air-raid. Minnie moaned at 2.30 am and I woke up. I stuck my head through the black-out curtain in time to see a mass of flame floating down in the sky, not far away. Everything around was lit up with an evil yellow light. We had to rush down to the shelter in our dressing-gowns, some with curlers and some greasy with magical formula night creams; one girl grabbed her box of make-up which had been sent to her the day before by her fiancé. We distinctly heard two thuds as the earth was torn open. We were complacent about the whole thing until we saw the extent of the damage the following afternoon. One of our favourite shops had been hit. The day before I had been inside this shop and bought some Elizabeth Arden soap, Lemonies. It occurred to me that they could have presented me with whole boxes of it - there was nothing left of the shop whatsoever except a smouldering heap.

The thought that I was to leave Hull was very cheering. It had not all been fun and friendship. There had also been depths of depression all of us had had to cope with: missing our families, monthly problems, strange diet and lack of freedom. We had also had two tragedies. A lively attractive girl in our cabin, who rushed everywhere as if she were on skates, suddenly became ill. She died in hospital only a short time afterwards - we were told from jaundice. Then Wren Flux, in the next cabin to ours, became seriously ill. She had had a fearful cough for some time, which kept the rest of her cabin awake, but suddenly she left the Wrenery and the news came that she, too, had died.

Before leaving I went to stay once more with Dr. and Mrs. Milligan, carefully signing the overnight book this time. They lived in Hessle, just outside Hull, and had three daughters: Diana was in the ATS, Mary in the Land Army and Helen, the youngest was shortly going to join the Wrens. I was given Diana's room, pink with flowery chintz covers. Mrs. Milligan felt I ought to have a long sleep with all those night duties and insisted on bringing me breakfast in bed. There was home-made bread, eggs, home-made plum jam and lovely creamy milk, and the pretty china matched the room. The contrast with Navy issue mugs and Wren breakfast was picquant, every delicious detail was like a birthday present.

The Milligans were a wonderful family and made me feel like an extra daughter. On one afternoon I was shown some of the family treasures, including a lock of Beethoven's hair, given to Mrs. Milligan by her great aunt, a musician who had lived in Germany. They were a highly organised family, were scandalised when I helped wipe up and popped the knives and forks straight back in the drawer - they had to be polished with a special cloth first. They also taught me how to iron a shirt properly - double parts first, sleeves, then all round.

There was another air-raid warning that night. I awoke to see the full moon looking straight in at the window. I heard a plane overhead and some guns firing but I was so warm and comfortable in that delightful bed that I dropped the blackout curtain and went back to sleep.

Before I said goodbye to Hull I received an invitation to attend a commissioning party. This was to be on board an armoured tug which had been built higher up the river Humber at Goole. We drove to the Goole shipbuilding yard and went on board a stocky little craft, looking like a new toy straight out of the box. The cheerful crowd on board was a mixture of her Navy crew and the men who had built her. Amid much rejoicing and plenty to drink we proceeded in a dignified fashion down river to dock in Hull. We were allowed to take the wheel in turn, while a rather agitated member of the ship's company advised us where to hold the smooth wooden spokes, surprisingly heavy to feel and yet light in response when an adjustment had to be made. There were no dramatic orders like 'Hard to Port', just a minor correction here and there and then 'Steady as you go'.

As I stood there feeling like a real sailor at last, I thought it odd that women could not do some of the jobs at sea and share the dangers. I had been conditioned to think of the sea as a man's world and that women on board would be too much of a nuisance or too much of a diversion, or both. What I did not realise was that about this time Dame Vera was busy thinking along these lines and that her ideas would affect me directly.

10.

It was September and the river at Greenwich looked remarkably like a Canaletto painting of it.   There was the same warm and delicate colouring of the houses, people, ships and over all a gentle haze, only the periwigs and fichus were missing.   And here I was again, not a lowly nobody on a teleprinter course but sporting a white Cadet band round my hat.   What larks.

But it was as well to be absolutely on tiptoe, we could very easily be sent back to base literally, hitting a snake's head and - zoom - back to where we started.   At least I was not now afraid of saluting the wrong person, although I think we were still secretly amused: there was inevitably something of the musical comedy about it.   However, we appreciated that a salute was a respectful gesture;   we were acknowledging a superior position and accepting his or her right to tell us, if need be, to go and jump in the river,   one just had to hope it would be a warm day.

Superintendent French was in charge of the course and welcomed us all on arrival.   She was stately, slim and kindly, with rolls of little grey curls on each side of her face.   She was quietly authoritative but also friendly.   I admired her on sight and my admiration grew during the training course.   She managed to calm the nervous and to draw out of everyone their best.   She had no rough corners.   Her combination of womanly grace and strength of character made her an ideal person for the job of handling course after course of potential officers.   I never saw her angry but I think she could have been formidable if anyone had failed to keep to her high standards of behaviour. She somehow managed to learn every single name of the forty cadets within a day or two of our arrival.   During the first week she would make a point of speaking to every cadet at least once, often stopping one of us when passing on the stairs and saying "Now, let me see, you're So-and-So".

Superintendent French also gave us our first lecture on the history of Greenwich, originally called the Palace of Placentia. Henry VIII was born there and we were told it was he who had started Trinity House for the chartmakers and that "we are still the greatest chartmakers in the world". Her lecture was about how proud we should be of our power as a sea-going nation. Just what was needed to stiffen up the sinews and summon up the patriotic blood of each new group of women who were to be turned into leaders. I made notes and wrote out in full her closing words . . . "The Royal Navy, with its abstract spirit that is so strong, understands that the world must aim for SECURITY, JUSTICE, TOLERATION".

A First Officer gave us a boring lecture on gas. The only way to listen was to imagine gas floating in at the window.

"When fitting respirators the eyes must be centred; if the face is marked at the sides it is not fitted correctly. The centre valve must be kept free of moisture and the exhale valve must never rattle".

We were told not to keep things in the gas mask case "as DAMAGE can easily be done to a vital part" and, a certain air of reproach came in here, "sections of the respirator cost the government *forty-five* shillings." (Of course everyone did keep things in their gas mask cases, where else would one keep powder and lipstick?)

We were also informed, rather worryingly, that the gas masks were *not* a protection against - leaky gas mains, sewer gases, carbon monoxide etc. We noted down religiously the rather strange order we might have to give:

"Gas masks slung - string fastened, flap open. Hold straps and PUT ON. Adjust straps to head."

The possibility that one might be an officer in charge of a group of people dependent upon one's remembering the correct sequence of the order in an emergency was worrying. It was slowly dawning on us that having other people's lives under our care was a sobering thought. Who knew where we might be sent or in what dramatic event we might find ourselves.

There was a lot of first aid: treating concussion, epileptic fits, drunkenness, etc. For drunkenness we were advised to "make the patient sick with mustard and water, putting the head to one side to prevent vomit being inhaled into the windpipe". Heavens! A drunken Wren or a drunken sailor? . . . heave-ho my hearties.

There was advice under the heading "Office Routine" with suggestions that we should study the character and background of any head of department we might find ourselves under, the better to adjust, since some men - it was always assumed they would be men - might differ in their preferred routine. We were advised to be "tidy, materially and mentally, seize opportunities, have pigeon-hole minds and the right outlook", (not stated but assumed). The lecturers used a lot of musical similes, harmony in the work place and so forth, and above all we had to aim for simplicity of routine. "Remember, complications increase work. Think of your successor - keep it simple." And a quote: "Give us the facts and cut out the cackle." Winston Churchill.

We learnt a lot more about pay and allowances. Our pay as Wrens had been adjusted to the nearest florin "below that which was due, the balance being withheld by the Paymaster, which balance formed a bond against desertion . . ." in which sad case ALL that money would be confiscated. Officers would be paid to the nearest pound. There was also a war bonus of eight pence per day (Admiralty Fleet Order 4500/42). I wonder what happened to that?

There was, delightfully, a Harmonium Allowance, paid to anyone who performed this duty for Sunday Service and/or Sing Songs. Wedding dresses were available on loan should these be required.

We ran from lecture room to lecture room; it seemed the next lecture was always in another building, up or down flights of stairs, back and forth across the open space between the two arms of the Palace. About three minutes were allowed between lectures. We could just make it at the double. I wore out one pair of shoes completely.

The background noise of Greenwich, apart from the ubiquitous pigeons, were the trams. They were the first sound that woke us in the morning, and if we couldn't sleep they seemed to rattle and clank and hum and screech all night. I believe they stopped at midnight and resumed again at five a.m, but the rumbling must have been recorded in my subconscious.

Towards the end of the three week course we had talks on the part women might play in the future. There was obviously

51

some government dismay at the level of education of women. The Markham Committee had made an enquiry into all three of the women's services and found a frightening lack of education which, in anticipation of the position of women after the war, had to have something done about it. We were told that adult education in the future had to be made more attractive to combat lack of interest and, as far as the forces were concerned we, as officers, would be expected to help counteract ignorance.

How were we to help? Apparently we should form discussion groups. We were advised to take an easy subject with beginners, we must try and persuade everyone to say something, however small. A example was given: "whether it is better to eat in the dining-room or the kitchen" (sic) - just the thing to get everyone going in scintillating style. We were told to invite outsiders, have comfortable chairs and offer refreshments. As potential leaders of discussions we were told to watch the quieter people and draw them out and to sit on the too confident. We were advised to use the Army Bureau of Current Affairs and the Weekly Intelligence Reports, using our nous as to what could be a good subject for discussion and what was secret and therefore dangerous. We were told to "control the use of the wireless". (I disagreed with this very firmly but not audibly.)

It was slightly mollifying that the Markham Report appreciated that a great many women had had to leave school early to join the services and were missing the chance to study for higher education. I wondered if the lecturer realised how very uneducated a lot of us were; we must have made this clear sometimes by the questions we asked but it seemed we were given, outwardly at least, the benefit of the doubt.

It is interesting that it was thought necessary to counter Hitler's New Order - his racial and economic theories - which might influence the uneducated. All the people I had come across so far were fervently against these ideas already, but I supposed their Lordships knew better.

When lectures finished at half past six, we raced back to our cabins to have a quick wash and brush up before dinner. Breakfast, lunch and dinner were in the awe-inspiring Painted

Hall, begun by Sir James Thornhill in 1707. It had been planned that navy pensioners should eat there and while he was at work on the vast ceiling the pensioners dined in the rooms underneath. The Hall was completed in time for George II to install officially 1500 pensioners. In 1778 there was a fire in the chapel and most of the dome and interior were damaged. They were restored by John Stuart. I imagined the pensioners, in blue coats, cocked hats, blue shoes and stockings, entering the Hall. I wondered what they had thought of it as it was more like a cathedral than a cheerful mess.

On entering, there is a flight of steps from left and right which meet together on a platform. From there more white marble steps lead up into the great hall itself. It was possible from this vantage point to see to the far end where there was a raised platform with a table for the senior members of the College and staff. Down the centre of the hall were three very long tables. We had to wait until the signal was given by the Chief Steward to proceed to our places. While waiting we went to collect a napkin in a ring with a number on it, which was kept in a honeycomb stand with hundreds of little numbered holes which corresponded to the number on the ring. At the time I wrote:

"We stand in little groups of classes and each newcomer threads his way to a familiar face. We chat, our eyes straying towards the tables. There is a lot of subdued noise at this end of the hall while we all wait, but in the vast dining area an orderly silence as a steward, male or female, in white gloves, glides about adding a last minute salt-cellar or straightening a glass. The light from the tall candelabras set at intervals along the length of the three tables gives a magical atmosphere to the hall. In peacetime, the ceiling chandeliers are lit, but apparently the blackout is not quite good enough. This is highly dramatic as the lights on the tables shine down on the glasses and silver and the background is lost in shadow. From where we wait, the huge hall is cavernous and mysterious.

"The dark uniforms are very becoming in this light to nearly all the women; above the navy serge, the white collars and glimpses of white shirts draw all the light to the head and hair.

All the shades of hair colour can be seen, all clean and well-brushed, from pale gold through all the shades of brown to black and occasionally, standing out like a torch, a head of red-gold or even dear old 'carrot'.

"The Sub-Lieutenants, also doing a training course, are a little self-conscious and would-be haughty, with their new gold stripe.   It is amusing to catch them unawares as their eyes stray down while waiting to admire their resplendent sleeves.   The Midshipmen, RN, with the white shoulder tabs are also cadets. They are a trifle less exuberant than usual.   The vastness of the hall, the dignity of the College, all the gold braid about and perhaps also the presence of women in what was once a sanctuary for the male - a hitherto unbroken tradition where no women were permitted except on the odd formal occasion - all this has subdued them a little and they stick together, all of them looking boyish and very well scrubbed.

"The RNVR Midshipmen (Royal Naval Volunteer Reserve) seem anxious to fit into their new surroundings.   They are older than the RN midshipmen and look at us Wrens as women and not as some strange herd of creatures grazing by mistake on a private field.

"We are all of us absurdly on our dignity and conscious that we are being observed.   Have we OLQ (officer-like qualities)?   When the Chief Steward finally gives the signal with a wave of his glove we stream forward: Sub-Lieutenants and Midshipmen to the table on the right, Wrens to the centre table, RNVR to the left."

We had been told to go to the far end of the table and take up the next free seat, no choosing where you would sit or with whom.   A number of the staff would sit at various spots and you might land up next to one of them.   I soon discovered that their places corresponded to the candalabra.   You had to be quite alert and look ahead to avoid this without seeming to do so.   It was all a game, but a serious game.   Sitting next to members of staff we were in the firing line, so to speak; who knew what black marks we should get if we used the wrong fork or left a food ring on our glass.   We had compared notes on our fears and had probably blown them up.   I thought one would be much more likely to get a bad mark if we were seen to avoid sitting next to staff too obviously, or failed to talk and keep one's end up if we landed someone in the luck of the draw. Much more hair-raising was the thought that we would have to pass examinations and remember everything we had been told. If there was also a Maths exam I was finished.

As we sat listening to a lecture on the Administration of a Wren Unit, we were aware that on that day, September 29th, the Prime Minister, the Right Hon. Winston S. Churchill, was giving a speech to a gathering of six thousand women. He was reminding his female audience that the forty-six million inhabitants living in Great Britain and Northern Ireland were engaged in total war and that; "This war effort could not have been achieved if the women had not marched forward in millions and undertaken all kinds of tasks and work for which any other generation but our own - unless you go back to the Stone Age - would have considered them unfitted . . ." (He was learning - he had originally opposed giving the vote to women.)

He also said: "War has taught us to make these vast strides forward towards a far more complete equalisation of the parts to be played by men and women in society".

I would like to have been there to hear his growl as he rolled into full spate against "this monstrous Narzie engine of tyranny, cruelty, greed and aggression . . ." Whatever is now said against Churchill by the sober historians sifting through his political actions and noting his follies, nobody could have stirred the war-time soul of the average Briton better than this master word spinner and brave, dogged fighter. It is possible to rehear some of his recorded speeches but to anyone listening to him at the time, especially when his words came crackling over our wirelesses, the hairs rose on our necks, our scalps tingled. His spit-fire call to arms was almost sublimated into a physical clenching of the fist; he put an electric current into us all.

I am not sure we have quite lived up to him, but here is the closing part of his speech that day to the six thousand women:

"Freedom will be erected on unshakeable foundations, and

at her side will be Right and Justice; and I am sure of this, that when the victory is gained we shall show a poise and temper as admirable as that we displayed in the days of our mortal danger, that we shall not be led astray by false guides either into apathy and weakness or into brutality, but that the name of our dear country, our island home, will, by our conduct, by our clairvoyance, by our self-restraint, by our inflexible tenacity of purpose, long stand in honour amongst the nations of the world."

Stirring stuff.

The end of the course came quickly and the exams were upon us. We were not told how well or badly we had managed to answer the questions but some, not all, were informed that they were to be commissioned as Acting Third Officers. Several of us were to report to Portsmouth for training in cypher officer duties. We were given a week's leave. We were there. We had made it.

Now we had to be fitted for our new uniform. A friend of mine wrote some years' later, when I told her I was trying to remember everything about Wren days: "Oh the magic of the famous tailors coming down to Stoke Poges: Austin Reed, Gieves, Moss Bros . . . feeling that delicious doeskin cloth and weighing up which one to choose - 'Always get a *good* coat and skirt, it will last longer.' Being fourth in a family (a Vicar's daughter) and brought up in the war, I'd never had so many new clothes."

The Palace at Greenwich received a direct hit very soon after our course and the Officers' Training Course had had to move to Stoke Poges, but my friend was right about the doeskin; it was a minor miracle to leave behind the Pusser's serge and have a properly cut uniform.

The literally crowning triumph was that hat. Whoever designed it was a genius. It suited nearly everyone I ever saw in it.

11

The hazard was that we should think ourselves as born again and become puffed up at the sight of that unimagined glory, one blue stripe on our sleeves. Wrens now saluted us and *we* did the acknowledging. It was an invitation to pomposity, but luckily there wasn't enough time to get properly inflated. There was also the thought of having to take responsible action at any time, which we had been prepared for and which could be waiting round any corner to catch us out. Before time and custom had quite taken away the excitement, though, we revelled quietly and had our photographs taken, which went up on mantelpieces and a few grand pianos in different parts of Britain.

On leave there was a moment of shock when a Chief Petty Officer, a seasoned, deeply-tanned old sea dog, saluted me suddenly in Lower Regent Street. Metaphorically I fell over backwards but just managed to return his salute.

Reactions to the war at this date, October 1943, could be summed up as optimism overlain with anxiety. The Russians were gradually beating back the German invasion of their country and the Allies had landed at Salerno in September, reaching Naples on the first of that month. There was to be no easy victory in Italy since the Germans were not to be dislodged without great sacrifice. We did not know then that it was to be a slow and painful campaign. However, the Allies were at last on European soil, Mussolini had been superceded and Italy had joined the Allies. It was just a year since the Battle of Alamein which was for most of us, after the Battle of Britain, the psychological turning point of the war.

Portsmouth and Chatham were the two largest Naval establishments. In 1939, when Vera Laughton Matthews and Angela Goodenough had visited both places to find out how the newly formed service could assist, they were well received at Chatham and given lunch, but at Portsmouth they were not taken very seriously. However, that lack of perception on the part of some senior officers was long forgotten and Wrens were part of a huge establishment. As well as all the usual jobs as drivers, dispatch riders, boats' crew, signals officers, cooks, stewards, writers, etc. they were cleaning and testing guns in small boats (a category known as Q.O - Qualified Ordnance) and Ships Mechanics L.C. (Landing Craft) and Torpedo Wrens, all given the same training as the men. Naval Control Officers went on board merchant ships to brief the captains on convoys and changes of route, confidential books were kept up to date, charts corrected, and the Fleet Mail Office was entirely manned by Wrens, including taking out the mail boat to all the ships in harbour.

Part of our course included going into the Signal Distribution Office in Pompey. The volume of signals being dealt with was astonishing. The place was cavernous and nerve-racking. I wondered why I had ever wanted to be sent to Portsmouth and put in a grateful prayer for Hull. It had been possible in a small place to get some idea of who everyone was and what their jobs were, here one would feel like a blow fly on an elephant corpse. But I had a sobering thought: I might be sent to a similar demonic forge of people and machines. Small place or large, nowhere was likely to be ideal and - sternly calling myself to order - it was the war effort that mattered.

While learning cyphering we were put up in the Wren Officers' quarters in Southsea. Here there was a bit of unexplained magic, or a premonition, whatever you care to call it. Another newly minted officer called Marjorie and I were staring at the stretch of water in front of us, watching the comings and goings of many different ships. It was abuzz with movement. It was fascinating and we did not have nearly enough time to stand and stare. Suddenly we both saw the unmistakeable turret and cigar shape of a submarine passing before us. Our eyes were glued to it. It moved slowly and impressively. Later, when we compared notes, we had both had a strong notion that whatever job was ahead of us it would be to do with submarines.

"Great events (for us) cast their shadows before". We were both appointed to Submarine Headquarters. Whatever the magic was, neither of us, so far as I know, has been able to forecast a Derby winner.

Flag Officer Submarines (FOS) was a rum sort of naval establishment. It had taken over a block of flats at the corner of Finchley Road and Fitzjohn's Avenue at Swiss Cottage. It was just possible to visualise its bulk of several storeys as a large ship defiantly floating south towards Avenue Road and Regent's Park. The main entrance, guarded by naval personnel, was on the Fitzjohn's Avenue side where now unending streams of traffic mount to Hampstead. We never knew what had happened to the people whose flats had been taken over. How much notice had they been given to get out?

The Cypher Office was on the fourth floor. It was a large room which had once been somebody's sitting-room. There was a room next door for the Wren signallers and teleprinter operators for whom I had a fellow feeling. It took me a little time to realise that I was supposed to be decyphering in the big room and not working with them on the machines. There was a shaky amateur lift which took us up for our periods of duty. The Wren Officer in charge was First Officer Lady Page Wood who refused to use any lifts. They tended to break down, she said, if she ever got into one, and she did not intend to be marooned for the rest of the war locked between floors.

A third room in our "flat" was a wireless room, manned by ratings, and the kitchen was almost continually in use for making cups of tea. The tea was made in a large naval issue green and cream kettle. The tea was brought to us in the Cypher Office. It was so disgusting that I asked the rating responsible how he made it.

'I put in eight tablespoons of tea, then a couple of tins of condensed milk, then the sugar and pour on boiling water. It's OK, isn't it, Mam?' It seemed too churlish to criticise. 'It's fine; thanks.' It almost put me off tea for life.

When we went "on watch" it was with five or six other Wren officers, one of whom was the officer in charge of the watch. These seemed to be very intelligent folk, with two rings (Second Officers). They were without exception very helpful and courteous. The team who worked together tended to make firm working partnerships, as had been the case in Hull. If one had to change watch for any reason it was a nervous business until one had got used to the ways of the new Head of Watch and been accepted by the other members of the group. Time may have coloured my spectacles but jealousies, nuances of behaviour, taking exception to tones and remarks, all the complications that arise when groups of people work together, were at an absolute minimum at FOS. The individuals had been welded into teams, perhaps by luck, perhaps by good management, and we had something of the spirit of the British Rugby team taking the field against the All Blacks.

There was a lot of laughter. Humorous stories were carefully hoarded and retold. People cut out jokes from newspapers and pinned them on the green baize noticeboard next to the Admiralty Fleet Orders, Regulations and plain language signals. There was one cartoon cut out from Punch. It showed a submarine dressed overall with the crew's washing. The Captain, standing by the periscope, provided the caption: "Right, chaps, down we go for a final rinse", I am sure this had been pinned up by Roly, an exuberant character who operated a joke network. Whenever she had a spare second she typed out and duplicated her jokes which she then distributed to the members of her far-flung naval family.

As new arrivals, Marjorie and I were taken to "make our number" with the various heads of departments. Lady Page Wood made sure that we knew who was who. This was an excellent scheme of introducing a new bee to the hive and ensured that we did not feel complete strangers for long. When we went down at morning break, or at teatime, to the wardroom on the floor below we felt part of the whole group, and soon we were relaxed enough to be able to exchange conversation or banter with whatever gold or blue braid happened to be there. We were, in all but physical reality, joining a ship. It was essential to have a closely integrated team in order to have a happy and successful ship. Refer to Admiral Nelson for the inspired development of this belief. With the exigencies of war, women were now included in the team, for so long an all-male preserve. In most places where tact and intelligence were to the fore, the transition was a smooth one.

October 1943. On my first watch I was plunged straight into the aftermath of one of the most daring exploits of the war. An Admiralty communique announced that the battleship Tirpitz had been damaged by midget submarines at her anchorage in a Norwegian fjord.

The Tirpitz was a sister ship to the Bismarck which had sailed into the Atlantic and destroyed the battleship Prince of Wales and the battle cruiser Hood in May 1941 before being sunk. It was feared that the Tirpitz would also emerge to wreck havoc in the North Atlantic. Like the battle cruisers Scharnhorst and Gneisenau, the Tirpitz had been moved to Norway and was anchored either at Trondhjem or Alten Fjord. Its presence there was a threat to the convoys taking war materials and food to Russia. The "Arctic" convoys as they were called, sailed on average once every two weeks to Archangel or Murmansk. In 1942 Churchill promised Stalin that he would step up the convoys, to the Admiralty's dismay. Because of the threat of the Tirpitz it was decided that if a German surface force appeared, the order was to be given to the convoy to scatter and the escorting ships to withdraw. German planes spotted the convoy, No. PQ17, and sank four ships. The order was given to the convoy to scatter since the air attack coincided with the Admiralty intelligence that the Tirpitz was about to put to sea. The merchants ships were told to make their own way to Russia and as the convoy broke up the U-boats moved in to the kill. Of the 35 ships, 24 were sunk. The Tirpitz had not moved; the threat had been enough.

For months top secret training and preparation had been afoot to develop the "midget" submarine and the human torpedo. They were expressly designed to attack large ships holed up in "safe" anchorages which were too difficult for ordinary craft to penetrate. The midget submarines were manned by crews of four, the human torpedoes with a crew of two in diving suits; the aim was to dive under a target, fix an explosive charge to the bottom of the ship and get away before the charge detonated.

The officers and men had been specially selected from volunteers for "special and hazardous service". Some were submariners, some were not.   Before departure, Admiral (Submarines), Rear Admiral C.B. Barry, DSO went to inspect the crews about to face a thousand mile trip in rough seas before they reached their objective, the battleship Tirpitz, securely guarded at the head of a narrow fjord sixty miles from the sea and protected with a huge net cage.   He later described them as "like boys on the last day of term, their spirits ran so high".

On September 22nd three of the X craft, as they were called, commanded by Lieutenants Cameron, Henby-Creer and Place reached their objective.   Three of the craft somehow got through the enemy minefield and made a passage up the "long, vigilantly patrolled fjord, past listening posts, nets and gun defences.   They reached the Fleet anchorage and got inside the anti-submarine and torpedo nets only 200 yards from the Tirpitz; then from a position inside they carried out a cool and determined attack.   At least one of the submarines was sighted and so close was she to the Tirpitz that those on deck of the battleship opened fire on her with small arms.   The submarines disappeared and shortly after there was an enormous explosion that lifted the huge bulk of the Tirpitz several feet.   When the confusion subsided the Tirpitz was no longer a fighting unit.

"On board the battleship there was intense activity, alarm bells ringing and orders being shouted; guns were fired and depth charges dropped.   The submarines were still within the nets and could not escape.   Lieutenants Cameron and Place scuttled their craft to prevent them falling into the hands of the enemy, but before doing so they took every measure to ensure the safety of their crews, a majority of whom, together with themselves, were taken prisoner.   Nothing is known of what happened to the crew or the craft commanded by Lieutenant Henby-Creer.

"Two V.C's, three D.S.O's and one Conspicuous Gallantry Medal were awarded for this operation, which for persistent daring and endurance is unique even in the annals of the Royal Navy."   (From the official account published by the Admiralty.)

12.

Captains of submarines tended to be very young, it was said they were too old at thirty-five. They usually sported beards and had the demeanour of being modestly but incontrovertibly the jewels in the naval crown. They were very sure of themselves, we observed. They had been tested and their nerves were strong; they knew their job. There were only a few seconds after viewing a possible target through the periscope to decide tactics. No margin for error. Decisions had to be made rapidly and accurately. In their charge was one of the most elaborate and deadly instruments of war. The company of hand-picked officers and men had to have total confidence in their youthful captain. These men often had about them an air of mystery, a knowledge of an element they knew and we did not.

Gradually we began to appreciate their particular problems. We knew that they had to surface in order to send signals and to recharge their batteries; this period on the surface was hazardous as the Germans might get a fix on their position. Weather interfered with the signals they sent and radio conditions were often far from good. We also knew that in the cramped conditions on board it was not easy for the officer responsible, the Sub-Lieutenant, known as the Fourth Hand, to code up a signal. Mistakes were easily made and one wrong figure of a group could throw out the entire meaning of the signal. "Corrupt Groups" were often received, sometimes quite a number of figures were missing and we could not always get a "check and repeat" until too late for the signal to be any use. A lot of our time was spent, detective fashion, trying out dozens of combinations that might possibly make sense. It was said that women were better at this painstaking business as they did not lose patience as easily as men did. Those of a stubborn temperament did well. Some of us felt challenged by corrupt groups, there seemed to be a demon there laughing at our inability to make sense of the puzzle. We had to try and get it or bust.

Sitting in our warm, blacked-out office, unspeakable tea appearing at our elbows at intervals, it was important to imagine the impossible conditions at the other end of each signal. Those submariners encoding their signals were imprisoned in a tiny, smelly, tinny cell under the sea, deathly quiet - noise could be picked up by the enemy if a concentrated search was going on over their head, depth charges could explode at any moment - no wonder, too, that when they surfaced at night the telegraphists should occasionally send the odd incorrect figure. It was our responsibility to read their minds.

One captain, reporting an attack, waited seven hours while sixty-two depth charges were dropped. His report was laconic: ". . . little real damage beyond lights being smashed and a few small leaks."

When the air-raid warning sounded we had to race down to the basement where a duplicate signals' room, cypher office, etc. had been set up. The duty officers who ordered us below were usually submariners, on their way up for promotion or being "rested" and most regarded the job as tame while the real war was going on elsewhere. Some did not bother to hide their annoyance at being balked; their hearts were in the dangerous metal tubes under water, and being in charge of the movements of their associates, who were their friends or rivals, was irksome and made them fretful. Some of them had very different reactions and we had to get used to their vagaries. One night, as the siren sounded, one Duty Officer, lean, bearded and worried, would order us to get below immediately:

'Don't wait for anything, just get down there.'

The following night it might be the other type, perhaps more used to responsibility, more relaxed, or perhaps more devil-may-care. There was one humourist who always wore a white sweater, its length encasing a nascent paunch, who would appear and tell us we had better make our way downstairs.

'Take the books; that's all I worry about, *you're* expendable but I'm damned if we can risk the cypher books.'

We varied our pace accordingly. We preferred to collect the books, the signals we were working on, and check quickly that we had everything we needed so that work could go on undisturbed below. The thought of sitting in that stale cellar with nothing to do was higher on one's list of priorities than

64

imagining a stick of bombs just being aimed at the block of flats. Not bravery, more like stupidity, but we had all had to work out our own private reaction to possible danger, and some of us were fortunate, we had not seen anyone injured or killed and had only our imaginations to cope with.

The cellars were horrible. There was no room to spread out our work properly and we sat between metal walls of large filing cabinets and equipment. It was noisy, damp, smelly and claustrophobic. There were beds behind the filing cabinets where we could snatch a nap if there was not much work coming in on night duty, but when the All Clear sounded and we went off duty, the relief of walking out into the fresh morning air was sensational. The world was full of bird song and beauty. There were usually few cars about at that hour of the morning and the short walk back to our Wrenery off Avenue Road was a sparkling delight, quickly dispelling the tired eyes and dead-stomach feeling of night duty.

The house we had been allocated in Queen's Grove had once belonged to Princess Mary, the Princess Royal. It was a modest but comfortable house, smaller than the grander houses in Avenue Road, most of which were boarded and shuttered for the duration. These empty houses had rather an embarrassed air, as if they were ashamed that their owners had scuttled off to safety.

We felt we were in total luxury. Our wardroom was pleasantly furnished and our rooms had beds, not bunks. We each had a wine account, just as if we were officers on board ship, and we could sign for drinks for ourselves and visitors. There was a small shop, called the Canteen, run by one of the officers, where we could buy soap, chocolate and so on. These items were stored in the basement in an enormous walk-in safe, once used, we imagined, for the Princess Royal's jewellery.

The Dramatis Personae were from all over the British Isles. There was the aforementioned Roly, who never walked quietly anywhere. Her feet were always placed heavily and pitilessly over the polished floors and were maddening if some of us were trying to sleep. There was tall, elegant Stella and her friend Jennifer, with whom she shared a nice wry humour, and Midge, who lived up, or rather down, to her name, being very short, full of roguery, with an uncensored view of life that was quite educational. She had a very large number of boy friends who seem to have bought, smuggled or somehow procured for her make-up of every kind. This hoard, that rivalled Selfridges' beauty counter pre-war, was kept in a cardboard box under her bed. She was very generous with it and several of us profited from her treasure chest. She was one of nature's business women and the only one among us, I am sure, who had her own income from pre-war enterprise.

There was Angela, poised and beautiful, who should have been photographed for a Wren Officer's poster. Her aunt was Gladys Young, the much loved actress whose exceptional voice and acting ability had made her into radio's Grande Dame. She was famous not only for the memorable parts she had brought alive in radio drama but also for her humour and strong moral personality. She was one of many interesting guests who came to the house. At lunch on one occasion I sat next to her. She told me she had now reached the happy position of being able to choose the parts she wanted to play. She had just rejected a part in a Somerset Maugham play. 'I've decided never to act in a play by him, his work leaves a nasty taste in the mouth.' I was mystified, but was much too shy to ask her why. Somerset Maugham's homosexuality was not generally known then. He was much admired by military and naval types who would, like my father, have thrown away his books in high horror if they had known the truth. This fact Maugham appreciated very well, rejecting later pressure on him to be frank in a more sympathetic age.

Gradually we all became aware that something very big was being planned. Some of the heads of watches, who had decoded certain signals, already knew that it was part of the great build-up to the invasion of Normandy. Some of the material we were dealing with was directly or indirectly connected. We know it was going to happen but not how or where. We rarely even discussed it on watch but from very soon after joining FOS until 2 a.m. on the 6th June the following year, 1944, we were in a state of suspended excitement all the more powerful for being suppressed.   We were conscious of a huge pot quietly on the simmer which would come to the boil in the good time of our captains and generals.   Our part was miniscule, but it was vital that everyone got through the daily test of one hundred and twenty per cent speed and accuracy.   It was, I suppose, the closest the whole nation had been to working towards a single end.   In or out of uniform almost every citizen in Britain, with Canadians, Americans, New Zealanders, Australians, Free French, Dutch, Poles etc. had their minds fixed on the inevitable, the real challenge to Germany which had to be on French soil.

The codename Operation Overlord was known to a few only.   The fewer who knew the safer for all.

There were easier subjects to discuss in the Cypher Office. "Monsters" had come up.   This was the code name for the big ocean-going liners such as the Queens, Mary and Elizabeth, the Mauretania and others which had been pressed into war-time service to bring over American and Canadian forces to Britain for the huge build-up to D-Day.   Vera Laughton Matthews had been successful in her campaign to get Wrens doing useful jobs everywhere, even at sea.   The buzz went around that Wren officers were wanted to handle the decyphering of signals sent to these big ships.   The liners were manned by their peace-time crew of merchant seamen, who, not coming under military discipline, could not have access to Naval codes.   Naval personnel had to be appointed for this duty.   Dame Vera suggested to their Lordships that it was folly to waste naval officers who could be more usefully employed and that there was no reason why Wren Officers should not take over this job.

In the book "Blue Tapestry" Dame Vera wrote about the gradual change that was taking place in official thinking.   She used to try and listen to the Parliamentary debate on the Navy Estimates, for which notes on the WRNS were prepared, giving statistics and details of new developments.   The debate in 1943 had been of particular interest when Sir Stanley Holmes, MP for Harwich, moved an amendment recording admiration of the part played by the WRNS and proposing a still further extension of their activities.

The Civil Lord of the Admiralty, Captain Pilkington, made a reply to the amendment, stating that the WRNS had become a "real, living integral part of the Royal Navy". In reply to a suggestion that Wrens might be employed at sea he said 'I have no doubt that if you gave the WRNS a chance, they would be perfectly prepared to sail a battleship'. What was of more importance to Dame Vera was his next statement that there was no Admiralty objection in principle to the WRNS serving afloat.

Whatever the mutterings at the time about women being on board with several thousand men, the pure fact that finally counted was the shortage of male naval personnel and it was at last thumbs up for the Wrens.

A list went up in the Cypher Office at FOS calling for "Monster" volunteers. A column of names appeared. There were so many from the two watches who had had the chance to read the notice first and sign, that by the time our lot came on duty it seemed almost pointless to add our names. However, I signed.

In due course the list shortened despite the fact that each Wren officer appointed was allowed three trips. Staff were posted to other places, got married, had sudden commitments at home, went on one trip and were seasick, or just had cold feet. Jennifer and Stella blazed the trail. Jennifer met James Cagney who was sailing with the American Forces. She told us, completely lost and starry-eyed, that she would never look at another man again.

Names on the list moved up. One morning I was bidden to First Officer Lady Page Wood's tiny office and told to proceed to Liverpool to join RMS Mauretania. It had happened. I had a ship.

13.

At Queen's Grove I flew about like an ecstatic bluebottle. Stella and Jennifer, who had each done three trips, gave me a detailed briefing and helped me to pack. They had returned loaded with goodies for us all and as the next one with the golden short straw I began to make a list of other Wren officers' requests, noting stocking sizes for nylons, special creams and lipsticks and so on. When I asked Roly what she wanted she said 'Bring me an orange.'

The family gave me a modest list but it included one item which might prove difficult. My sixteen-year old brother, John, was building his own recording machine in our attic and he needed a microphone; I had to try and find an RCA ribbon mike, the latest American design and unobtainable in Britain.

I was instructed to pack tropical shirts and a skirt. It was late July and not very warm in London so I wondered why. Stella warned me that New York would be sweltering. 'It's the same latitude as Madrid, ducky. You'll boil. Also, there's another reason.' But she didn't enlighten me.

It was almost too exciting and also frightening. Supposing I was laid low by seasickness, as others had been, unable to stagger on duty? Rattling up to Liverpool this was my chief fear. It was not much comfort to remember that Nelson suffered abominably from seasickness. Overcoming a physical disability is not my forte. There were no anti-seasick pills available then, only my grandmother's expensive advice that champagne was the perfect cure.

Reporting to Flag Officer Western Approaches, a title of splendid sonority, the Duty Officer told me which dock the ship was in and the name of the Wren Officer from another base who would be sailing with me. There was a duty car to take me straight to the ship.

I had never seen, and certainly not imagined, any vessel as large as the Mauretania. From the dock she seemed gigantic. The side of the ship I could see, up to the first portholes, was like the Bank of England. In spite of her bulk her lines were graceful, her bows elegantly shaped. As I went on board, a dock worker standing on a platform slung from a deck called out to me cheerfully 'Hello, my dear. Got your life jacket?' 'You bet,' I called back, though in fact I hadn't.

The sights, sounds and smells of dockland were a powerful welcome: fishy, oily and full of the shrieks and whooping mockery of gulls. Stores were being loaded and the cranes ground and squeaked as they moved over the ship's hold and back again, swinging the cargo precariously in frail-looking nets.

Up the gangway and into a new element, hard to pinpoint but different, set apart. Nobody in uniform seemed to be about. Then an RNR Lieutenant appeared. He whistled up a steward to take my suitcase and show me to my cabin. The decoration and elaborate fittings of the ship made it instantly clear that she had been built for comfortable cruising. There were signs: First Class Only, Bar, Cinema and so on. The cabin for the two Wren officers was on the Sun Deck, with a porthole. It had its own shower. I wondered how much it had cost in peacetime. There were two fixed bunks, the one under the porthole appeared to be unoccupied while the other was piled with clothes; it looked as if someone had opened a suitcase and tipped everything out. When I met Elizabeth, the other Wren officer, I discovered this was exactly what she had done. Elizabeth had already been on one trip and was therefore senior to me. She was friendly and helpful and the untidiest person I ever met.

Elizabeth had already worked out our rota of duty and she took me along to our "office", a tiny narrow cabin fitted out with a working bench, two swing seats and a lockable cabinet for the code books, signal pads and so on. We were next door to the Wireless Room. Here were the powerful transmitters and receivers with large dials to turn to pick up signals from far and near, indicators galore, and keys like small taps for sending morse signals, and all the paraphenalia of a modern warship's communication equipment of those days crammed into a small area about the size of a small bedroom. The space left for the five or sometimes six men on watch seemed miniscule.

Later I was taken round the ship to meet some of the staff and to make my number with the Captain. We were to sail early the following morning. I walked round and round the various decks to try and find out where I was, often quite a mystery. I enjoyed barging through the FIRST CLASS ONLY signs and exploring wherever I dared. This was now *my* ship and I had to get my bearings.

Looking over the side I saw that a number of army officers and men were drawn up on the dock. On certain sharp orders the men crashed their boots down as if trying to make cracks in the dockside and there were a lot of smart stiff leg and arm movements and more echoing incomprehensible orders. Then we realised that this army contingent were escorting German prisoners of war. As they marched on board under escort I looked at the prisoners closely. Most of them were grey in face as well as grey in uniform. The exception was one tall man in a long greatcoat who held his head high and looked round him proudly and scornfully. He looked just like the Junker, jack-boot type we had hissed at in so many propaganda films. One of the British officers later told me that he was a stiff-necked customer, a Nazi General, who had informed them that it was only a matter of months before Hitler's secret weapon would bring the Allies to their knees. My feelings were mixed: it was difficult not to admire his courage in the circumstances but this thought got quickly submerged by loathing. His sort had meted out too much death and destruction for charitable consideration.

All that day people in different uniforms streamed on board. There were RAF and Fleet Air Arm personnel on their way to Canada and the United States for training, some nursing sisters and one or two important-looking civilians who hurried on board, and sometimes off again, not looking to right or left. One of them turned out to be a King's Messenger. He showed me the little insignia under the lapel of his jacket. I wondered if, like the messenger in Alice, his name began with an "H".

The bustle and excitement was just the same the next morning. Knowing the exact time of sailing and not being needed in the Cypher Office, I hung over the deck watching everything.   It was too exciting to miss a thing.   Then all visitors were ordered ashore, the companion way removed and ropes cast off.   The engines had been turning below for some time but now there was a gentle movement away from the landing stage as the tugs pushed and nuzzled at us.   The Liver Birds on top of Liverpool's famous building began to slide away.   England was being left behind.   There was a moment when we wondered if we would, all of us, return.   There were a few dock workers to wave us goodbye.   We all shouted and waved back.

I believe it was Sam Goldwyn, sailing from New York some years ahead, who shouted to his friends on shore "Bon voyage".   I understand his confusion;   it is a dramatic business, leaving by sea, no stations or airports come anywhere near the excitement.

That first night the huge ship seemed to get a sniff of the high seas with a sort of glee.   The green water began to race past the portholes and I discovered what it meant to be on a totally blacked-out ship, not a light anywhere.   It was just possible to make out the cranes and other machinery in the bows, then nothing.   Everything was battened down.   It was very silent.   Only the ships' engines churned and spun out the white wake aft.

To avoid a torpedo attack from a lurking U-boat, Mauretania went at a very fast rate of knots, changing course frequently to prevent a German getting a fix on us.   In the asdic room the needle swung, producing green blips as it passed land or a lighthouse or a ship in the vicinity.   It was hypnotic to watch, this small magic pool of different shaped elipses which had to be interpreted correctly or our lives would be at risk.   I was thankful not to be responsible for reading sense into those green shapes.   It seemed only too easy to miss spotting something which could not be accounted for by the charts and could be an enemy submarine, surface ship or attacking aircraft.   We were rather a helpless whale, noisily alone in that large ocean.   We would be dependent for five days   on   the   alertness   of   our   asdic   ratings.

On the first day I felt dizzy; the time on duty seemed very long. How did one set about finding a pair of sea legs? The old hands told me to eat. Off duty, I lay on my bed, watching the cabin dip and recover, feeling lightheaded; the thought of eating was quite impossible. Liz brought me some plain bread and chewing this did the trick. Thereafter everything was fine.

We were expected to appear in the First Class Dining-room for a huge breakfast, lunch and dinner, served by the overworked stewards, Mauretania's peacetime staff. They were a friendly teasing group who took a pride in serving us with the same style and panache as though we were passengers on a cruise.

About two days out, four of us were seated round a table for breakfast. The table was stacked with cereal bowls, jugs of milk, coffee and tea pots, eggs, bacon and toast. As it had been relatively calm, the four-inch high protective edges to each table had not been raised. Suddenly I saw the dining-room and our table dip away from me in the most alarming manner. Everything on the table began to slide. With a split-second sauve-qui-peut I appreciated that what goes down will come up, and I leapt out of my chair sideways as the entire contents of our table came hurtling to where I had been sitting and landed on my chair and on the deck with a diabolical crash of breaking china. The same thing was happening to every table, the noise was awful. Several people rushed out, their uniforms dripping with milk, coffee, tea and bits of cornflakes. The amount of china broken was appalling. We had hit a freak storm. Thereafter, every table had the sides firmly fixed in position, but we went rather short of cups and plates until our New York turnround.

Now I found out why we had had to bring tropical uniform. We were to sail quite far south to avoid U-boat patrols and it began to get warmer. I loved to stare at the sea when I had time; the elephantine bulk of Mauretania made huge bow waves curve backwards, casting up spray and exposing a translucent undertow as the water was sucked back. It looked like boiling froth and green sherbert. Gradually the sea changed colour from all the shades of green to a deep rich blue. Pieces of yellow seaweed floated by. We had reached the Gulf Stream. Tropical kit was the order of the day.

It was getting hotter by the hour and oppressive out of the breeze caused by the movement of the ship. We used to rush into the dining-room at meal times and beg for ice water. Our special steward, Bill, made a joke of this and brought us jug after jug of ice water. On one occasion he put eight jugs on the table. 'Hello. You've only drunk one. What's wrong?'

The change into tropical uniform improved everyone's appearance. The men wore shorts with long white socks and white shoes and had white covers to their caps. They told us sadly that when we docked in New York they would have to change back into long trousers if they went ashore as shorts were not approved wear in the USA.

Liz and I found a good place to sunbathe when we were off duty. This was up a ladder on top of a ventilator. Perched up there with a rug and pillow we lay gazing up at the funnels, reading or just dozing. It could have been a luxury cruise.

Every evening someone gave a cocktail party to which Liz or I were asked. Part of the fun was seeing the huge suites which had been allotted to the very senior officers - some had staterooms of vast size, with bedroom and bathroom attached, fitted cocktail cabinets, attractive pictures, matching sofas and armchairs. It was easy to imagine them filled with flowers, champagne and attendant photographers when a film star arrived to cross the Atlantic. These staterooms had catered for some famous people. We had some interesting people aboard, too. One was a Mrs. Stewart taking her two children to the Bahamas where her husband was the temporary Governor while the Duke and Duchess of Windsor were away, and there was an American girl with a Southern Belle accent who turned out to be the daughter-in-law of the Lord Mayor of London.

'I'm not popular with my in-laws,' she drawled slowly. 'I surely am thrilled to be goin' home. They kept tellin' me to be sure to be ready on time, but I'm not made that way. I can't hurry and they got mad at me when I kept them waitin' . . .'

I could imagine the Lord Mayor's fury at this Southern charmer upsetting the stopwatch timing required to get through a Lord Mayor's engagements. I wondered if this had caused difficulty with her marriage. Her husband was not mentioned.

The place to go for a good argument was the Wireless Office. The operators were, to a man, as pro left as they could be, with at least two paid up members of the Communist Party. When there was nothing much happening, we enlivened the hours of watchkeeping with discussions on every subject under the sun, which somehow ended up with the haves against the have-nots dilemma. Occasionally there was some acrimony but on the whole they regarded me with a kindly tolerance as just another right-wing idiot. I advocated strongly that business should be given its head after the war in order to raise the standards of everyone, my father's argument which I had adopted, not having many ideas of my own. This point of view was not heard much then and they doubled up with laughter. My reputation was of an argumentative blue goose and I was usually greeted with the clenched fist salute whenever I went into the Wireless Room, or left it. I mocked the signal back at them. I wish I had known the Up-You-Jack sign but I didn't.

14.

So we had entered a man's world and no mistake. We had joined a ship's company of two hundred men but we had a job to do and were accepted. There did not seem to be any resentment at our presence, rather the reverse. Perhaps this was owing to the sensible behaviour of those who had blazed the trail. Also this was a merchant ship, built for cruising and well used to women about the place. It was not a ship of the Royal Navy, where women on the ship's complement then might have caused problems. We were included in the order that members of the crew did not have to carry life jackets, as all the passengers were ordered to do at all times. This clearly marked us out, to those who knew the rules, as part of the ship's company. On the return voyage this fact was not appreciated and caused problems.

As naval personnel the Wrens were under the direct charge of the Senior Naval officer on board, a Gunnery Officer, RNVR, in charge of various armaments, installed on a peacetime ship hopefully to ward off air and sea attack. At fixed times there would be gunnery practice when the Lieutenant Commander and his team would poop off enthusiastically to see if everything worked efficiently. During these times, every member of the ship's company not required on deck, and all the passengers, were ordered below. I used the excuse that my father had been a Gunnery Officer in the First World War and got permission to stay on deck to watch, promising to keep discreetly out of the way. It was very cheering. There was first the nervous rat-tatting of the alto Oerlikons, firing in staccato fashion at imaginery German or Japanese aircraft and then the sudden shattering bass roar of the big gun, built on a platform above the place where a swimming-pool sparkled in the sun in peacetime. There was the feeling that the great ship, built for pleasure and now busy with her own war effort, just *might* give back a thing or two on her own account if she were attacked. The violent noise, the reverberation and shock to the ears were a kind of physical sublimation of one's hatred of Hitler.

Our "landfall" was to be early in the morning. We knew our approximate time of arrival and it was too exciting to sleep.

My imaginary vision of New York was of cloud-topped Illyria but there was something stronger than the much photographed skyline in my thoughts. Throughout the war, our American Aunt Ellice had kept our spirits flying with occasional parcels of butter, usually rancid by the time they arrived, and a blissful toothsome sweet from a Boston shop called "Crunch". More important, perhaps, than the edibles was the weekly New Yorker magazine, food for the imagination. We could see from these pages that there was a place where women and men still dressed in elegant clothes of beautiful materials and we pored over the advertisements of places like Saks and Maceys and Abercrombie and Fitch; the names were very well-known to us and represented another world. We had also enjoyed the wry, intelligently funny and penetrating comment on life and affairs in the famous editorial. We had revelled, too, in the view of Britain at War, written by Mollie Panter-Downes, who interpreted *us* to *them* in so many clever articles which, obliquely, taught us about America. I knew very well that I was about to enter a magical new world.

Some of us stood on the highest open deck below the bridge. Mauretania moved forward gently, dipping and returning, her movement accompanied by a merry ringing of the bell buoys which had been set dancing by the slight breeze and our bow waves. The sun, rising in the east, had just appeared at the stern and it floodlit the windows of all the skyscrapers ahead of us so that the city seemed to be competing to reflect the sparkling golden light. How high, how incredibly high, were those amazing famous buildings which came steadily closer. What had been the thoughts of those first architects who had dared to challenge gravity like this?

We rushed to the port side to observe the Statue of Liberty, awed by the American ideal of freedom extended to all who came to these shores: "Give me your poor, your hungry . . ." I could not help thinking of the German prisoners, unable to see the Statue from their confined quarters below.

As this amazing city grew larger and nearer we could see that it was already astir. The yellow taxi cabs were carrying their fares to start the world's business. We could just make out a line of them waiting by Pier 90, our small slot in the great river, towards which we were now being slowly edged, our own engines silent. We began to be interested in breakfast but it was too exciting to move. Ahead of us now was our berth, complete with a notice with the ship's name on it; it made me think of a well-kept stable with the horse's name painted above it. We watched the pilot, wearing a lightweight suit and a broad-brimmed summer hat. He kept shouting instructions from the bridge as gradually, very very gradually, we were eased into this small water stable.

It was on a much later arrival in another "Monster", when the New York tug captains were on strike, that the English captain brought one of the Queens alongside this very pier entirely unaided, to the worried amazement of the American Port Authority who had advised docking in the river. It was a great piece of skilful seamanship considering the size of the ship and the narrowness of the dock area allotted to it.

Now that we were at the toes of the skyscrapers, the whole thrust and power of New York seemed waiting to engulf us. New York must be one of the most dramatic cities to arrive at by sea because you land right in the heart of it. Standing beside me watching were an English naval officer and an American army officer. The Englishman knew all the sights and pointed out the Empire State Building, Rockefeller Center, the Chrysler Building to the chagrin of the American who couldn't have helped. He told us *he* could tell us everything about London.

The Coastguards came on board to photograph everyone going ashore in order to issue to each a special pass. I held a card under my chin for the picture and felt like someone accused. Next we all lined up for the fingerprint man, with a black pad in front of him. He did not speak at all but seized my index finger, rolled it on the pad and on to a piece of paper. Not content with this he proceeded to roll every single finger on both hands, finally even the palms of my hands. I wanted to ask him why this was necessary as I understood *one* fingerprint was sufficient and wasn't this a fearful waste of time with all the members of staff and crew waiting to go ashore? However, I thought it wise to shut up in case we were held up any longer. We had already had to wait an hour and there was a long line behind me . . .

It was getting warmer by the minute. The stiff white drill and the shirts with shoulder tabs to show rank, were smart but a trifle unyielding, but I was thankful for the short sleeves. I was actually walking down the gangway at last. What to do? Find a telephone. My Aunt was the only American I knew. I could not have written ahead to warn her I was coming as, obviously, the whole movement of the ship was secret. Beyond telephoning her I had little idea of where I would go or what I would do. I just had to see a bit of America. I had four day's leave and some dollars. These I had not really worked out in "real" money nor had I any idea of what anything would cost. A really green Limey had arrived.

The dock was busy, cabs and trucks and people all going somewhere. Someone told me where to find the nearest bar. Inside I was faced with a telephone which was different. How did it work? This was all very embarrassing, a simple task and I was stymied. I couldn't make sense of it. I asked the barman.

'You need a coin, sister,' and he slapped the required nickel on the counter. 'Want me to show you?' Retreat into female helplessness was very easy in those days, no-one had given us any guilt about it. 'Yes, please, would you? That would be very kind.' My accent seemed to turn the bar upside down. Early morning customers stared at this peculiarity in a strange uniform. They seemed to be a bit wary of me as if I were a species of animal life that no-one had yet classified.

When I got the operator I asked for Ellice's Boston address as I did not have the telephone number. The operator found me the number very quickly and after some minutes I heard a quavering voice on the line.

This could never be my six-foot, red-haired, dynamic Aunt, even though I had not seen her for eleven years. 'Hullo, operator, something's wrong. Is that the right number?'

'Well, the body said she was Mrs. Endicott.'

The body? On reflection I believe the operator called her the "party" but I misheard her and the voice did sound as if it was on its last gasp. It added to my anxiety. 'Please try the number again . . .' This time the ringing tone stopped and a soft voice answered my question. 'Mrs. Endicott is not here. She is away on holiday in Cape Cod.'

'Is that Ellen?'

'Yes it is. Who is this?' It seemed strange to me that Americans prefer *this* to the English "who is *that*?" Is it because the Americans are more immediately friendly whereas we British like to keep people at a distance until we know who it is? I explained who I was and Ellen, my Aunt's maid, who had been with her since her marriage to Billy Endicott, gave me Ellice's telephone number in Cape Cod just before my money ran out. I got another lot of coins from the barman. Everyone was getting interested and several people offered to get the number for me. It occurred to me that if I couldn't contact Ellice I should have to find a hotel somewhere. This time there was a well-remembered voice on the line.

'Aunt Ellice? It's Angela, I've just . . .'

'Is that my niece from England?' She was very quick on the uptake.

I explained I was in New York and had a few days' leave.

'Go get a train from Grand Central station, there's one about noon. It'll take five hours. Get out at Woodshole - got that? - Woodshole, and I'll meet you. Don't bother to bring a thing. I have everything you need here.'

Slight panic was dispelled. It suddenly seemed a wonderful idea, quite normal, to get a train to a place called Woodshole, Cape Cod - where was Cape Cod? I thought it quite remarkable that Ellice should have cottoned on so quickly to who I was. Last time she had seen me I had practically been in the nursery. I tried to remember everything I could about her. As a small child she had once told me that in her house in the country, outside Boston, there were fairies in her garden and she had seen them. I could remember believing her absolutely. This time she had the key to a more grown-up fairyland.

Her husband, Billy Endicott, had died some years before. I remembered that he had looked like Edward VII, plump, bearded, beautifully suited and smelling of cigars. He had lost a great deal of his fortune in the 1929/30 crash. There were so many bankruptcies and disasters and Billy used a lot of his own money to help many whose savings were lost. We had been told as children that Billy Endicott was a man of high principles, scrupulously correct in everything he did, even to the extent of declaring his bridge winnings on his income tax returns, which seemed to us to be slightly overdoing it. He had, earlier, paid for the training of Helen Keller, the girl who was born deaf and dumb. He was a great American gentleman of a past age.

He was also the last person who controlled my aunt.

What was the time? Half past ten. I had just time to do something very important. I hailed a yellow cab. It could have been Cinderella's golden coach.

'Pardon me,' said a voice before I could get in. 'But what is your uniform? Are you from England?'

I stopped with my hand on the cab door to explain that I was a Wren, part of the British navy.

'That is great. How are things back there? We want you to know that we are right behind you good people and admire you all so much . . .' There was quite a group of interested people and I felt like a celebrity. We all shook hands and I thanked them. Apart from the barman these were the first New Yorkers I had met. I was warmed by their welcome and spontaneity.

'Fifth Avenue, please,' I said to the taxi driver. There was a card displayed with a photograph of him. I added 'Mr. Levinsky,' as I supposed the card had been put there as a kind of introduction. He turned round and began to ask me questions about the war. His accent made it hard to unravel what he said. I slipped in a question myself: 'How far is Grand Central . . .?'

'I thought you said Fifth Avenue, lady?'

'Yes, I did. I want to go to Saks and then I have to go to Grand Central Station. I have to catch a train at 12.0 o'clock. How much time should I allow?'

'Leave it to me, lady, I'll get you there. I'll wait for you at Saks . . .'

'Oh, I don't want to go inside. I just want to see it, as much of Fifth Avenue as possible, please, if it won't cost too much.' 'It won't cost you much,' he said. I wondered what his idea of much might be.

'Could we also go down Broadway - if it's not out of the way?'

A cartoonist would have drawn me with eyes far out on stalks. The immense buildings made the streets seem like narrow passages. The pedestrians were very controlled after London's casual ways of nipping across a road when you spotted a gap. Here there were WALK and DON'T WALK lights manipulating everyone like marionettes. Everything I saw looked luxurious. Everything that people wore looked attractive, new and colourful. The sun shone; the windows of Saks were as elegant as I had imagined. There was Tiffany's . . . and there at last we were underneath the Empire State Building. I got out to stare up at it and felt like an ant below a giraffe. My neck ached.

I don't think he can have charged me the proper fare. It seemed very little. I added a dollar, hoping this might be an acceptable tip and thanked him.

'I plan a visit to London, England, when the war's won,' he said.

Grand Central was grand indeed, a green marble vastness with a ceiling almost out of sight. It was the hub in those days of great journeyings and had not been condemned to second class status by the aeroplane. Black porters were moving across the scene like rare beetles with their red caps, the rest was a hive of people. I found a row of discreet-looking ticket offices and bought my ticket without using my brain. I discovered I had bought the most expensive seat, First Class, the seat a revolving armchair in a carpeted luxury carriage. On the return journey I travelled with the daughter of a millionairess who saw to it that we travelled third and paid less than half.

The outer suburbs of New York sped by smoothly. There were hoardings advertising wonderful things. The swing chair was a pleasant idea and with the whole of a wide area of carriage to oneself it was easy to adjust to any point of view. Suddenly one of the other occupants of the carriage got up and handed me a heavy bundle of newspapers.

'This your first trip over here? Take a look at our noos.'

It was the New York Herald Tribune. It weighed pounds and was absolutely endless, twelve or more separate newspapers, each one treble the size of a paper at home. There were also about a dozen bulky magazines and supplements.

'They say a whole forest is destroyed to print one edition of that,' the kind donor told me, rather proudly I thought. Primly I thought it a terrible waste, yet from the narrow world of rationing, where we tried not to waste anything and got fined for throwing away bread, it had a certain panache. I thanked him very much and settled down to try and read some of it.

It was hot. There was no air conditioning then. A tall steward came by calling for lunch bookings. He suddenly said to me rather nastily 'You're British, aren't you? Your country stinks.' Shocked, I looked at him. Was he German? He was very good-looking. What had got into him? 'Look what you've done to Ireland,' he said. Ah ha! So that was it. 'I haven't done anything at all to Ireland,' I said, shaken by the surprise attack. 'You're all bloody responsible,' he said.

My newspaper donor and his wife, with whom I had got into conversation across the wide aisle, asked me to be their guest for lunch. Their son was in the American Forces overseas and they had a lot of questions. I felt grateful to my kind hosts for the meal but I was more grateful for the protection of their company. The handsome steward, balked of the chance of another attack, gave me a sneering smile when he came to our table. I thought afterwards that what we would now call his body language had been in direct opposition to his remarks.

Five hours to the minute from New York we pulled into Woodshole Station. Instructed by my self-appointed guardians, I walked along the corridor to the point where I could alight, as the train was too long for the small station. Passing through the carriages I could see people lined up waiting on the platform and when I opened the door, by amazing chance, there was Aunt Ellice standing precisely opposite me, wearing a sleeveless dress, her famous dark red hair in a spangled net with a black velvet ribbon on top. Here at last was my godmother, the donor of wonderful gifts throughout my childhood, my father's favourite sister.

15.

The meeting was joyous. She smelt of expensive perfume and looked very handsome, if unusual. She strode along as if no-one else existed, which for her they possibly did not. She went for clever, talented or famous people and had little time for the rest. I knew I was on trial. It was slightly alarming. We walked in the afternoon sunshine to her station wagon in which she had piled things I might need, including tennis clothes. We drove at once to a tennis club.

One of Ellice's friends was Helen Wills Moody. Ellice herself was no mean performer on the tennis court. She had once been the indoor ladies champion of Massachusetts. Billy Endicott had built her an indoor tennis court so that she could practise daily. Now very alarmed I realised she wanted to try me out to see if I had inherited, obliquely, her talent. This was apparently of prime importance. We changed.

I like to think that my mediocre performance was due first, to having just got off the train after a five hour journey and second, having to wear the shoes she had brought along for me which had a slight heel and did not quite fit. I fell in her estimation. I was obviously not going to be eligible for those expensive lessons she had been planning for me when the war was over. She said I hit the ball like a man, which was some consolation. But the rest of my stay was enchantment.

Woodshole, on the Cape Cod isthmus, looks across blue water to the island of Nantucket and in the distance, the island called Martha's Vineyard. There is third island called Elizabeth Island. The story I was told was that a man once owned all three islands. As he had three daughters he gave the first to Elizabeth, Martha had the second and as for the last, his youngest, Nan, took it.

We swam, sunbathed and went shopping for swordfish, caught just off the coast. I remember seeing a pile of discarded "swords" in a fisherman's hut and devilish weapons they seemed. The fish itself was delicious, like chicken fed with prawns.

Going shopping in a large store near Woodshole everything became more like a fairy tale than ever. Ellice insisted on buying everything I admired as well as extravagant gifts for the family. The nylon stockings were of a quality I had not seen before and there was a soft round-necked sweater of the angelic pink of the inside of a small seashell. She gave me perfume, make-up, dresses, underwear and a suitcase to carry them all in, as I had just travelled with my uniform shoulder bag. It was a heady pleasure to be out of uniform and in such pretty clothes.

She was staying in a house of New England style, with floors of polished wood and colourful rugs. Everything seemed to gleam and shine. The tiled kitchen-cum-dining-room had a huge old-fashioned stove. The windows of all the rooms had frilly organdie curtains of coloured spots on white and they looked new or as if they had just been washed, ironed and hung up. There was a green cover to the loo with white flowers on it which matched the bath mat. This was new to me. Nor had I seen matching towels, of every size, all stitched with initials.

On that first evening I met some of Ellice's friends and we had cocktails on the terrace. At dinner the helpings were so enormous that even my determined appetite weakened at such extravagant quantities.

After dinner, three of us walked to the village. It was my first view of a shop lit up at night; my reaction was one of alarm before remembering that here, on this side of the Atlantic, there was no need to be vigilant. Lights were everywhere: twinkling lights on the water from ships and, strangest of all, houses with lights streaming from their unblacked-out windows. Parts of the walk were quite demanding as one false step on a narrow path would precipitate one into the swirling canal. They warned me to watch out for poisoned ivy which gave one hideous and painful spots. When we left the roadway we had to walk in single file, led by one of Ellice's friends who knew every step. As we went along in procession, they quite gaily, me nervously for fear of poisoned ivy, an aeroplane, port and starboard lights very clear, came flying over the water and suddenly turned on a powerful searchlight. It lit up the entire area for miles and made a dazzling gleam on the inky black sea. It was like a photographic flashlight staying just long enough to get all the details.

Ellice's friends treated me like a celebrity. They all wanted to question me about the war. They asked me what my job was on board ship, how people were surviving the rationing, had I been in any air-raids . . .? They were eager for every scrap of information, which I had to strain to keep within secrecy limits without seeming to do so. The more understanding of the women in the group seemed to be embarrassed that they were living in such plenty when we were not.

On the last day before I had to return to my ship we were invited to tea by a friend of Ellice's. I gathered that in the realm of rich women she was in a league of her own. She owned a house right on the headland which had suffered from a hurricane some years before and it had been badly flooded. I was told to look for the water mark on the outside door and walls.

Ellice also gave me details of the occasion. She said it would be interesting and probably amusing as the lady was eccentric and kept an Irish poet to read to her. 'Look carefully at her pearls,' Ellice instructed. 'She will wear them, whether she has on a summer frock or a ball gown. She always does. You will never see pearls like those again.'

We drove up to the house. A summer holiday house? It was enormous. We rang a bell and the double-fronted door was swung open by a butler. Inside it was a Hollywood movie set, stuffed full with antique furniture, pictures and strange and beautiful objects. In one room there was the head and antlers of a deer and in the next room the rest of his body disappearing into the wall. It had been so well done that we were convinced it was about to walk through the wall from whichever side you looked.

It was really the Mad Hatter's tea party. There was a very large round table with eight or ten people seated round it with plenty of elbow room. The table was laid with delicious-looking cakes and "cookies" and all of us had an empty cup and saucer in front of us of very fine china. Although everyone talked, it was rather like being an instrument player in an orchestra as we all had to be controlled by the conductor; and the conductor was our hostess. Everyone deferred to her. Her poet sat on her left, playing the stage Irishman a bit, I thought, with a lot of blarney and bon-mots sprouting out of him whenever there was space in the conversation, very clearly aimed to please our hostess and amuse the company. It was an interesting link to the eighteenth century families in England who often housed and fed young men who were promising and whom they thought would add lustre to their house.

The tea ceremony appeared to be an unusual occurrence and I wondered if it had been specially arranged because Ellice and I were English and therefore could be expected to take tea. Our hostess stood at the table behind a large silver urn, calling out to everyone in turn for their tea requirements - Indian or China, milk or lemon, sugar or no sugar - and I observed that as she operated the urn, added a flick to the wheel of conversation here, called another cup in, brought in a guest who was not speaking, kept the topic of her choice dominating, wielded the milk and sugar, that every single guest was getting what they had *not* asked for. The lady on my left had asked for China tea with lemon and she got Indian with milk. I had asked for sugar and got none, and I observed the total muddle but, curiously, there was not one single demur. Everyone took their medicine and played their part and politely drank whatever had been put before them. I was amazed at my aunt, whose reputation had always been for saying precisely what entered her head. But I saw that she had embarked on a private conversation with the only personable young man there, until swept back into the main stream again by our hostess.

I looked at the pearls. She wore them with a fawn-cream dress that was, I thought, tussore silk. It was true - the pearls were very large and splendid. It seemed rather an odd notion to wear them on a hot afternoon on a summer holiday but I was obviously out of my depth here. I looked at those pearls as from a great distance, because I had been told to, and felt no wish to possess them, or any like them, which was probably just as well.

A quiet girl, sitting some way to my left, turned out to be the daughter of our hostess, Louise. She was about my age and was travelling to New York the next day. It was arranged that we should travel together. She was almost deliberately plainly dressed, had a serious and intelligent air and I guessed she might be reacting against the formality of her mother's house. She was a career girl and worked as an agent for musicians. On arrival in New York she took me straight to Radio City where she was launching a singer, a cheery, large black lady who may have become famous but, alas, I forgot to memorise her name.

I recall express elevators and long narrow corridors, a small office and studios with warning red lights outside: KEEP OUT. AUTHORISED PERSONNEL ONLY BEYOND THIS POINT. Louise and I were authorised, it seemed, and we sat in on the recording session. I was amused to observe the metamorphosis that had taken place - the timid home chrysalis had turned into a sophisticated New York fritillary.

Louise and her friend, with the wonderful name of Annie Laurie Chestnut, adopted me for the rest of my few hours in New York. We leapt into and out of cabs while they helped me to do my final shopping. I managed to run the ribbon microphone to earth via the kind advice of one of the wireless operators. I also remember buying something in Abercrombie and Fitch. It was astonishingly hot. There was no air conditioning, only a fan turning. The unfortunate man serving us had to keep his left hand to his brow with a handkerchief to catch the perspiration; when he released his hand to do up my parcel the sweat dropped on to my bill. I wondered how they could endure such conditions.

The shopping expedition was like last minute buying fever on Christmas Eve. All three of us took a cab to the dock so that I could dump my suitcase and parcels and make certain that shore leave was still until midnight. I then dashed off the ship again to the waiting cab and the three of us sped off for dinner to a restaurant called 'Theodor's'. It was still fearfully hot but it did not rob us of our appetites. The proprietor greeted Louise as an old and valued friend and gave us a brandy on the house. I felt I had been made an honorary New Yorker. I had been half in love with New York in my imagination for all the war years, now I was hooked for life.

I got back on board with about three minutes to spare and waved goodbye to Annie Laurie and Louise from the deck. With all the shops open late, I had more packages. Louise presented me with a box of chocolate Hershey bars and the refreshing "Candy with a Hole". It seemed I had collected an almost indecent amount but later when I compared notes with the others I found my mountain of loot relatively modest. The last purchase of all had been oranges and bananas. Our cabin was full to bursting, a chaotic mess of heavenly items.

16.

The next day was high frustration as we did not sail, but no-one was allowed ashore. New York could have been a thousand miles away. All day men and women in uniform came on board in what seemed a never-ending queue. I began to wonder how there would be enough space for all of them. In the evening I spent some time gazing at the lights in the skyscrapers and listening to dance band music coming from somewhere across the water, with the counterpoint of the imperious klaxon calls of the cabs. Lighting from a gymnasium in the dock opposite ours made a path of blue light across the black water. The call of life ashore was strong. Sternly, I went below to sort out some of the mess in our cabin.

We sailed the next morning. I watched the beautiful skyline again as long as it remained in view. The bell buoys rang us out as they had rung us in. The ship was completely packed with American servicemen and a few women. To move on deck was almost impossible, you just had to push between people or step over bodies. Getting anywhere on board was an adventure as there were endless attempts to chat us up. It also seemed a bit churlish to pass by. I stopped when I had time and admired boatloads of photographs of wives and families already desperately missed. All the passengers had to remain on deck during the daytime hours and could not return to their cramped quarters below decks. They whiled away the time by reading, talking and playing endless games of craps and poker.

There was one very hard routine which the American forces had to endure. They were only to have one big meal a day, presumably the only way that the food would go round. This the tough, steak-eating Americans found desperately irksome. Liz and I would secrete rolls, cheese and fruit in our pockets from our meals and hand them out discreetly to some of the men we had got to know. It didn't help much; we needed another loaves and fishes miracle.

Everyone had been ordered to carry their life jackets at all times. Owing to the varied number of uniforms about, the Wren officers' get-up was not familiar to the Americans. As I made my way about the ship I was continually being stopped by senior, and junior, American officers and asked why I was not carrying my life-jacket.

'I do not have to carry one, thank you.'

'Why the hell not?'

'Ship's company do not have to carry life jackets.'

'Oh, pardon me . . .'

This dialogue took place several times.　It was my introduction to Ned, a cheerful Chicagan.　He whistled at me as I was on my painful exercise walk, over and past hundreds of bodies, most just resting with their eyes shut to pass the time. There were always a lot of whistles but this had more of the French traffic policman's "Stop" about it so I looked up.

'What have you done with your life-jacket?' said this tall, blue-eyed Second Lieutenant.

'I don't have to carry one,' I said primly.

'You don't say.'

'I do say.　Crew do not have to carry life jackets except in an emergency.'

'What are you?　Are you as nurse?'　I explained that I was the equivalent to their WAVES.　He wanted to know in detail what I did.　I told him, jokingly, that his life might depend on my efficiency and we talked of other things.　The conversation ended with Ned saying he was starving, so I added him to the filched roll and fruit handouts.　Not much help but something. He was very grateful, all six foot three of him.　On several other occasions we discussed the war and he told me that it would all be over soon now that the "goddam Yankees" were coming. *They* would sort out our feeble attempts so far to do the job.

On the next night out, some time after dinner, I decoded the message:

"To the Captain, RMS Mauretania . . . U-boat in your vicinity, 15N by 42W."

This had to be got up to the bridge fast.　I double-checked the degrees, locked the cypher office and went in search of the Captain.　To get to the bridge, in complete darkness, one had to climb through a series of blacked-out compartments, made light-tight, so to speak, by heavy black curtains.　Between the last two curtains I had to feel my way up the companion way like a blind man.   Suddenly I was aware of the fresh air, that I was on the bridge, the holy of holies, and that there were figures standing about peering through the darkness.   I asked for the Captain and informed him that I had an urgent signal for him.   He did not, as I expected, step back through the black-out curtains to take the signal from me but instead asked me what it said.   With a horrified intake of breath - supposing I got the degrees wrong? - I repeated it to him.   This would not seem an achievement to most but I have never been able to remember figures. Luckily Mercury, the undoubted God of naval communications, stood by my elbow.

The Captain immediately told me to get a life jacket and gave the order for the ship's company to carry them.

It was electrifying.   There was a calm and orderly stir throughout the ship as everyone took up their action stations.   In the asdic room, the tension was like a taut wire and no-one spoke at all.   I went back to the cypher office wondering if we should get another signal.

I stared at the tightly fastened porthole and listened to the steady and comforting noise of the ship's engine.   We were really moving, the forward thrust through the water had greatly increased.   One sensed the concentration of everyone's thoughts on board.   If being condemned to death concentrates the mind wonderfully, I thought, then so does the picture of the two of us, the U-boat and the Mauretania, nearing each other in the otherwise lonely Atlantic.   It was rather too easy to picture the U-boat Captain peering at us through his periscope and ordering "Achtung, achtung, torpedoes ready . . ."   I thought that if we had to jump overboard I must remember to unlace and kick off my shoes . . .   The despised, rather dirty white life jacket might be useful after all.   We were all, passengers and crew, literally in the same boat now.

We did not know how the position of the U-boat had been discovered and the warning sent.   It is possible that the U-boat captain was unaware that we were in the vicinity and had surfaced to send a message, which enabled his location to be pin-pointed.   Now we know that the warning came to us via the secret station at Bletchley where the German codes were broken. In those days we knew nothing whatever about Ultra. It made exciting reading long after the end of the war, and I felt personally grateful to the skill and vigilance of many, including my future sister-in-law.

Our arrival in Liverpool seemed to be very splendid. The voyage completed, here we were again, with a heightened sense of being joyously alive and not a bloated ex-person in Davy Jones' locker. The sea had turned back to green again and the sky grey, but it was home. Our main preoccupation was our goodbyes and how to carry all the stuff we had brought and get it through Customs.

There were various matters to attend to first, however, before going on leave. The confidential material had to be taken ashore and it was all tied up in a large sack by one of the telegraphists, a young and keen rating, with a wife and new baby, anxious to get on and get promotion. Just before we went ashore I noticed that he looked very unlike his usual cheerful self and his hand was shaking. To my dismay he confessed that one of the officers had ordered him to include six hundred American cigarettes with the confidential books. These were not, except in very special circumstances, examined by the Customs officers and it was therefore a safe place for smuggling. The telegraphist did not want to do it but had not liked to defy an order. The officer had already left the ship on leave and the bag had been sealed.

I felt coldly furious. If he were caught, the rating would lose all chance of becoming a leading seaman and his service career might be ruined. This was plainly a crime. If he said he had been ordered to do it, would he be believed? We all had trains to catch, there was not much time. What was my duty? I was clearly right in it.

I decided the only thing to do was to go ahead. It was too late to do anything else. I told Paul to stay right behind me as we went through Customs. I don't think I thought at all what I would say if challenged but I did promise Paul that I would see the said officer on the next trip and give him a very sharp piece of my mind. The words I would say to him to condemn his

93

despicable action in letting someone else do his dirty work got the adrenalin going. When we came level with the Customs officer I began a long spiel about all the things I had to declare. I took a quick look at Paul in the middle of this. He was standing behind me, the off-white sack on his shoulder, and to my horror I saw that his face was green. I had read of this in stories but had never believed it. The at-present benign Customs officer had only to look at him . . .

He passed my case, overnight bag, endless carrier bags, shoulder bag, humorously remarking that there couldn't be much left in New York. With what I prayed was a dead normal tone I said that we also had the confidential books and indicated the sack with a stage thumb jerk behind me.

'Books only?' he said to me, not looking at Paul.

'Yes.'

'Right. On you go.'

We walked as casually and unhurriedly as we dared towards the RN transport waiting for us. I hope those cigarettes gave the bugger cancer.

17.

A weight on all our minds while we were at sea were the VI's. Only two months before, in June 1944, the first of these were launched on London. At home we had been quite a target for bombers in our part of North London, the house next door to our's being completely destroyed in an early raid and our house declared unsafe. We had had to move. It was difficult not to be fearful despite my father's cheerful assurance that the odds against being hit twice were enormous. I tried not to think about it and get on with the job, but I found myself racing into the wireless office the moment the news was due in case there had been more VI's on London.

We did not know then that the V stood for Vergeltung - retribution. They had much the same effect as a snake, one felt hynotised to look for this pilotless aircraft tearing across the sky. They were twenty-one feet long and jet-propelled. When the throbbing sound switched off it was then about to drop its warhead of one ton of explosive on somebody. You were supposed to take cover immediately but it seemed fatally easy to remain rooted to the spot.

Back at Queen's Grove several VI's passed over us. One morning Stella, a girl called Anne and I were getting stores out for the canteen shop. The stores were in the walk-in safe in the cellar. Suddenly we heard the familiar sound of a VI. We stood listening, exchanging glances. Was it making for us? The next moment, Anne stepped smartly into the safe, pulling the heavy door after her. Stella and I were left on the outside, astonished. Then we laughed. We heard the cut-out, then the explosion, not near enough to shake the ground, and we told Anne the danger had past and she could come out. It had been an instinctive movement on her part but we teased her gleefully that she had had no thought at all for us. However, if we had been hit, she might have been enclosed in the safe for eternity.

The vital news we were all following with hopeful excitement was the progress of the battle in France. On August 15 the Allies landed in Southern France and on August 20th the Falaise gap was closed and 60,000 Germans trying to escape through it were captured or killed. On August 24th General LeClercq entered Paris. The only pity was that the attempt on Hitler's life in July, the bomb in the brief-case affair, had failed.

On our time off a new feeling of independence had grown. It seemed quite ridiculous that we should expect our escorts to pay for meals out all the time, when we were earning too. The first time I suggested paying my share of dinner the idea was regarded by an old friend, a bomber pilot, with great distaste. I had transgressed by stepping outside my proper role. He wondered what the world was coming to.

Here was a contradiction. At work, women had proved their usefulness and men had had to adapt to having them around, whether they personally liked it or not. In uniform we represented, hopefully, efficiency and common sense. The snide remarks which were passed in the early days of the war about women in uniform playing men's games had become fewer, at least they were mostly out of our hearing. However, off duty, out of uniform, old ways were reestablished. This was particularly noticeable in the pub, regarded by most men as being as sacrosanct as a club, where we women were by invitation only. A group of women on their own in a pub were thought of still as weird and unnatural. However, this didn't stop a lot of service women not giving a damn. Men, and escorted women, could think what they liked.

It was a great time for pub crawls. On one occasion we were out in a group and Sibyl, one of my friends from Queen's Grove, brought along her boy-friend, Eric Williams, whom she later married. He was the author of the famous escape story "The Wooden Horse". He had about him a high-wire tension that was exciting and slightly alarming. It must have been quite a crawl as I remember Eric using Sibyl's lipstick to write the word DUTCH in front of all the advertisements for COURAGE. We thought it hilarious.

But I had had the thought that it was absurd that I could not offer to pay for a round. All the women in the group were earning money, even if it was not equal pay - the expression had not then come into being - and that it was tiresome to be always saying "thank you" gratefully. Why should the men spend their pay on us all the time? It made one feel somehow second class. "Second Class citizen" was another expression that had yet to be born.

For my second trip in RMS Mauretania I felt a seasoned traveller, a proper sailor. I had a ship to join and I knew the work, what to expect and what was expected of me.

Catching the train to Liverpool again was as exciting as before. On board Mauretania it was almost a homecoming. As soon as I had dumped my case in the cabin I went to hug Nobby Clarke, the senior Radio Officer, and all my red cronies of the Wireless Office, make my number with the Captain and walk round the now friendly and familar decks.

There were no U-boats signalled. Unknown to us by now the Battle of the Atlantic had been largely won. The previous year, in March 1943, there had been over a hundred U-boats in the Atlantic, with thirty-two vessels sunk for the loss of only one U-boat. Now, with the Atlantic packed with ships bringing over troops and supplies, more U-boats were sunk than merchant ships. We did not have these comforting figures at the time.

On arrival in New York I telephoned Ellice again, this time at her home in Boston, and got my train instructions. Clued up, I avoided the armchair seats and, like an old hand, bought something to read and settled into my seat as if I had been commuting out of New York all my life. My uniform was again an introduction. People everywhere used any excuse to talk to me and ask questions about what it was like "over there". They were as warmly welcoming as ever but now, after two and a half months of the war in France - it was now August - there was a feeling of shared effort.

As before, the questions covered every aspect of the war. I hate to think how many times I told our personal bomb story but I remember they were the best listeners in the world. They hung on every phrase and admired my "accent". Head swelling stuff. The majority of people who came up to me in the street, in shops, or on the train, wanted to talk about the successes in France or to tell me about a relation's exploits in the Italian

campaign.   There were wonderful stories of the adventures of
their own sons and daughters, brothers and husbands, which
brought their heroes nearer home in the telling.   I learnt to
appreciate that asking *me* about *my* experience was often a polite
lead to the one really exciting story of the war.

Ellice was at Boston station to meet me, looking incredible
and, as always, drawing all eyes.   The world was her stage and
she dressed for it.   This time she had on a model dress from
Schiaparelli, printed all over with little heads in black with
different hair styles.   Her own, even redder hair, was tied at the
back with a huge twenties flapper bow. I adored her, she was the
most full-blown and fascinating person I had ever met.

We got into the shooting brake, talk spilling over with all
the messages and thanks from the family for the amazing
presents and the shared excitement at the optimism of the war
news. We stopped at a red light.

'That's strange, this light doesn't seem to want to change.
Something's wrong with it.'   She waited a while and then
decided to shoot the lights.

A little further on, on the same long street, the same thing
happened. We cautiously shot these lights too.

'My, my, what has gone wrong with these lights?'

At the third lot of red lights my aunt gave a wild shriek and
clapped her hand to her head.

'My God,' she said.   'I've lived here most of my life and
just today I forget it's a one-way street!'   There was not much
traffic that day or I would not be here to tell the tale.

We drove past an imposing brownstone house where she
and Billy Endicott had lived.   After his death it was too big to
live in alone and she moved to an apartment, as I was learning to
say, *on* Beacon Street.   The apartment was tiny but attractive,
part of one of old Boston's houses of the tea party period.   We
were to have lunch there before going on to her country estate.
After the war, when the Boston Strangler was on the loose, she
barricaded the place like Fort Knox but I somehow doubt that he
would ever have tackled her, even in old age.

'There's a hurricane forecast,' she said cheerfully.   'So I'd
like to get there fairly soon.'

We drove for some time. Gradually the great city and its terrifying freeways were replaced by suburban areas with wooden slatted "clapboard" houses. Each group of houses surrounded a New England church complete with its toy model steeple. There were green, manicured lawns, no fences between. I remarked on this, thinking it strange but pleasantly friendly compared to our fences and hedges.

'I've got a wall,' said my aunt.

Now we were in the real country and at last we entered a driveway and there was the famous house. It was at a place called Beverley Farms and I seemed to have been writing letters to Ellice here, care of the Post Office, for most of my life. Waiting in the doorway was Ellen.

I was shown to my room, exquisitely pretty in New England style. The fly screens at each window were the only nuisance as they impeded one's view of a huge garden below. My natural instinct was to remove one and stick my head out but remembering the warning about mosquitoes I thought better of it. Outside one window was an enormous tree.

Ellice's vast bedroom was entirely white, white walls, white furnishings, curtains and carpet. She had changed into a scarlet pyjama suit with a dragon embroidered across the left side and was lying on a white chaise longue. Scattered about the carpet were stockings, pants and the Schiaparelli dress. Ellen was in process of picking up these discarded garments. I was shocked. I had never known anyone with a personal maid and I thought it very odd to undress and just leave everything where it dropped. My mother would not have approved.

A few moments later Ellen reappeared at the door with an armful of Ellice's ball dresses. She was carrying a sheaf of net, taffeta, lace and silk in a palette of lovely colours. She asked me if I would like to try them on.

It was like being given the run of Harrods for the night. I tried on one after another, pirouetting in each in front of two full-length looking-glasses. When I reluctantly discarded one to try another, I had to stand for only a few seconds while Ellen expertly hooked, zipped and poppered me into each one. Being about the same size as Ellice, luckily they all fitted me well and I thought I looked amazing in all of them.   Some of them had very famous names sewn into them.   Before the war Billy and Ellice had made regular trips to Paris to keep her wardrobe up to date and she had had many grand occasions at which to wear them.   One dress, I remember, was a black velvet crinoline, the low neckline outlined with small pink roses and the front of the skirt was caught up with two larger roses to show the pleated frill of the under skirt.   I chose a sea-green taffeta dress with a wide frou-frouing skirt to wear for dinner.   Ellice looked out a necklace and earrings to wear with it and we swept downstairs for cocktails

On the radio the hurricane warnings were alarming.

"We advise you all to stay inside your homes.   Do not go out in a car.   Fasten all doors and windows securely.   Do not remain in a room with a large tree outside.   The hurricane may reach the area within the hour . . ."

Ellice seemed totally unperturbed.   We did a tour of the house to check all windows.   We had our cocktails in the drawing-room, filled with antique furniture, the chairs upholstered in a lime green that made an almost Chinese background for some red, gold and orange dahlias.   These dahlias had been grown on the estate and were the size of dinner plates.

In the panelled dining-room the refectory table was laid for two.   Opposite me was a portrait by Lely.   I questioned my aunt about it, was it an ancestor of Billy's, whose forbears had crossed from England in the Mayflower?   The candles were being lit, Ellen arrived with the first course and I forgot the answer.

Ellen put two strange-looking golden objects on the table.   It was Corn on the Cob, which I had never seen before.   It was delicious and dripping with salty butter which must have equalled a month's ration at home.   We had cut glass finger bowls to dip our buttery fingers in.   The beautiful china, glass and silver sent dancing reflections back from the candlelight.

Outside the magic circle of the dining-room we could hear the wind.   The trees all round the house were hissing and whispering in a way I had never heard before.   We drew back the curtains to look and the trees were swaying with a circular movement that was frightening. I felt more scared than I had ever been in an air-raid. Suddenly there was a loud crash and all the lights in the house went out. Ellen soon appeared in the doorway with another tall candlestick, holding her hand in front of the flame and looking like a ghostly parlour maid from some great Georgian mansion.

Ellice bounced up to make another tour of the house. She tried the telephone, which was still connected. She rang a neighbour and was told that a tree had been blown down across the electric cable at the entrance to the house. She seemed to be in her element. 'This house is much nicer by candlelight,' she said.

Later when it was time to go to bed she came with me to my room. The wind howled around outside as if angrily trying to get into the house.

'I hope you're not scared,' she said, with a throw-away note of apology. 'I think it's dying down a bit, don't you know?'

I didn't think so. The weird force out there in the darkness menaced. My imagination turned the house of brick and wood into a matchbox toy, us just paper dolls. The telephone was not working now. Supposing the full force of the hurricane swept across us? The huge tree outside my window would be blown into the room and I should be crushed in the old-fashioned bed as if it had been made of balsa wood. I kissed Ellice goodnight and said that of course I was not scared at all

Next morning we heard that the hurricane had blown itself away to the north. It had been given one of those friendly names like Dora, or Mavis - to make it seem less terrifying? On the radio news there was a long list of all the damage it had caused in the area. We toured the estate and found that the damage was limited to several trees down and a considerable destruction of plants and flowers. I had to rescue as many dahlias as I could to make a big display in the drawing-room for the dinner party which Ellice was giving that evening. I tried to make it "after Constance Spry", whose very first commercial arrangements were done at my uncle's gallery in London to disguise some bomb damage; the display was some way "after".

The enchanted time went all too fast. 'Call me collect when your ship gets in next time. I have a lot more people I want you to meet.' I had the feeling that I had passed some sort of examination. I never went to Beverley Farms again because our next voyage was to Nova Scotia and I could only speak to Ellice by telephone. A talented, vivacious lady, she was a little akin to Elizabeth I, tricky and dangerous if you put a foot wrong; that red hair was a warning. What was certain was that if you happened to be in her good books she was glorious fun to be with, witty, amusing and daring. The amount of money she raised for charity and for "Bundles for Britain" throughout the war, was phenomenal. In her later years she took up painting. While some unkind remarks were made about her canvasses, one of her 'beaux', as she called a number of eligible but ancient Bostonians, said to her "Everything you do sings". It was fair comment.

18.

At Flag Officer Submarines, "Northways" as the building was called, a new Admiral had been appointed. This was Admiral Creasy, CB, CBE, DSO, MVO. He had been Chief of Staff to Sir Bertram Ramsey, the Allied Commander in Chief, Expeditionary Force, where he had helped with the planning and execution of the naval side of the Allied Landings in France. The Allied armies were by this time sweeping onwards towards Germany and hopes were high that Hitler would be decisively beaten. Admiral Creasy had been appointed to FOS as part of the plan to concentrate the Navy's efforts in the Far East.

At this period no-one expected the German counter-offensive, which would begin in December, 1944. It was now September and the Arnhem operation was about to take place. The general atmosphere until that disastrous setback was of great good cheer. All seemed to be well.

With the new appointment there was a more relaxed air in the wardroom at FOS. I tried to pinpoint the difference and realised that the stage prop of my theory was the peanut butter. At tea-time and morning break, along with the jelly and jam there had always been a jar of peanut butter, about which a great many jokes were made. Originally, as a newly arrived, very junior, officer, it had been pleasant to discover that the "scrambled egg" brigade, those with a lot of gold on their sleeves, used jokes about the peanut butter as a conversational gambit. In the hierarchy of rank, it was slightly nerve-racking to be addressed by the top brass in a friendly manner; we were not used to it. The skill on their part was to put you at ease and what better way than a humorous remark about this American speciality, not known in the UK before the war. But we were never completely at ease. We were as much on trial when spoken to over tea as if we had been on parade. If a funny story was told, the right degree of laughter was of paramount importance; to roar with laughter or riposte too boldly made the Gods recoil. There was a slight, very slight, stiffening in their stance, a tiny note of coldness in the next, closing, remark. Yet to be nervous and not to reply at all was equally damning; one would be marked down as dull, unsophisticated or merely stupid.

Whatever had taken place in the past, however, Admiral Creasy had the Mountbatten touch. He was a man of charm and humour. He was dangerously easy to talk to, natural and encouraging, and one almost, in the interest of the exchange, forgot the height of the golden platform between us. The peanut butter ploy was no longer needed. There was another factor.

As the war progressed and thoughts of peace came up on the horizon the whole business of status, especially between men and women, seemed to be getting more complicated. There was a subtle difference of approach; some men were beginning to appreciate the fact that we might soon have to be thought of as just women again and not someone of a lower rank to be issued with orders. This was noticeable chiefly with the type of officer who was not all that sure of himself, in particular those who had had to work very hard for their rank and who were conscious of their achievement. Some in the past had even seemed to be scared of being too friendly with younger Wren officers; their position on the ladder and yours was the psychological barrier. Admiral Creasy's example set a new tone. We felt we were being treated as women first and a rank to command second.

There was also a reaction among us to being in uniform. The boredom of wearing the same clothes all the time began to seem irksome. Our hair, not supposed to touch our collars, was being grown by most Wrens just that little bit longer. We took more care of our nails and used discreet nail varnish. A lot of our talk was about our civilian clothes and the skills of some people in making utility garments look like models. Make-up was more available in the shops by this time, and although eye shadow and mascara were not supposed to be worn on duty, when we went out in the evenings we larded it on. The mascara then was a nasty little black cake which had to be spat upon to get any colour upon the tiny brush. It was a messy business and tended to leave flecks of black on cheeks, forehead and eyelids. Also the brush got clogged up and didn't do its job properly.

104

We borrowed each other's mascara and eye shadow to get different effects; unhygienic but friendly.

Lady Page Wood, in an attempt to make her Wren officer's hat fit more smartly, had cut out about two inches all round and sewn the top on again, making it very shallow. It perched on the side of her head like a black velvet pancake. Vera Laughton Matthews came to Northways on an inspection tour. On arrival she was clearly heard to say 'Haven't you done something to your hat, Page Wood?' 'Oh no, Mam,' she replied blandly. Dame Vera wisely did not pursue the issue.

There was a peacetime problem ahead but most of us had little idea of it as yet. On the one hand we were getting fed up with white shirts and navy blue skirts and jackets, and above all the weighty shoes; on the other we liked the work, liked the chance of using our brains and enjoyed the lively companionship on and off duty. Where, when the war ended, could we find such a worthwhile job and a job that offered such variety? We should also miss the exciting factor that we never knew what was round the corner, what we might have to do or where we might be sent. This added a spice to daily routine.

One afternoon on duty in the Cypher Office, I was summoned to Admiral Creasy's office. He had a small packet on his desk which had to be delivered urgently to the Admiralty. He told me to get a car and deliver it personally to one of the Sea Lords. There was no time to waste.

I felt lucky to have been on duty at such an obviously vital moment of the war. The Navy "four-by-four" with driver was already waiting for me outside Northways. I was out of breath, dashing down the stairs rather than wait for the weary ascent and then descent of the ancient lift. I leapt into the car with my precious package and told the driver to move.

He moved. We went at such a rate through Swiss Cottage, Regent's Park, etc, to the Mall that we made it in record time. Just in front of Admiralty Arch the driver very nearly killed us both, as he turned into the Admiralty building right in the path of a fast oncoming car which screeched to a halt within a centimetre of our paintwork.

Inside the Admiralty I was met by a cheerful Flag Officer.

'Oh good, you've got the flies,' he said. 'That's splendid. The First Lord has been waiting for them. He's off fishing. Convey his thanks to Admiral Creasy, won't you.'

Navy signals were graded according to their degree of secrecy and they had some spy thriller names. There was Confidential, Most Secret, Top Secret and, the best, Hush, Top Secret. The last one must have been thought up by a Smiley-type character with a nice sense of fun. Such signals were rare for us to unbutton as they usually went to the heads of watch. One afternoon we were very busy with a lot of signal traffic and I saw that I had a Hush, Top Secret to deal with. Before going any further I checked with the Head of the Watch. 'Go ahead,' she said. 'Decypher it and take it straight to the Duty Officer.'

The signal made it clear that another Allied conference was in the wind, that Churchill would be going to it and that it would be soon. There had been Allied Conferences already in Casablanca, Quebec, Cairo and Teheran; the last had taken place in November, 1943. The signal also requested three Wren cypher officers to attend from FOS.

Before the watch ended I was told by Lady Page Wood to go and see Admiral Creasy. I went along to his office, which I remember thinking was not really grand enough for him, though maybe it reminded him of a cabin at sea.

'First Officer Page Wood and I think you should be one of the officers to represent us at this Conference. Would you like to go?'

A breathless 'Oh!' and a quick follow-up 'Yes, sir.'

'You will also appreciate how secret this is. No mention of it can be made *anywhere* to *anyone*, no-one in your family, nor anyone in the Service, no-one in fact, outside this room. Now, let me see. You've been on three "Monster" trips so I think the best thing would be to say that you are going again to New York. That's the easiest explanation for your preparations and absence.'

It seemed no-one yet knew exactly where the Conference would take place. Our orders were to take plenty of warm clothing and, most interesting, to take civilian clothes.

'Well, I am sure the honour of Northways is safe in your hands and that you will do a first class job. If the news of this Conference were ever to leak out we can be certain it would not be through you. Good luck.'

He had that excellent combination of authority and inspiration that was reputedly the Nelson touch. I felt the chain of wisdom link back through time to the great Horatio himself.

I realised as I walked along the corridor back to the Cypher Office that my chin was in the air like a ballet dancer about to perform an arabesque. This would never do, I should give the whole game away by my ecstatic behaviour. I had to stop a moment to wipe off a grin which seemed to have joined my ears.

Off duty I had to go that afternoon to the West End. I sat in the front seat on the top deck of a bus and had a moment of delirium. The significance of being one of the very few to know such a secret burst into my brain. 'There's going to be another Allied Conference. Churchill will be going . . . and so will I.' The temptation to address the bus was wickedly strong, but of course I did no such thing. What was more difficult was to check the heart-stopping excitement of it.

More difficult was keeping a straight face as I told everyone I was off again to the United States and answering their questions convincingly. I decided that a successful liar must be a good actor; I had to pretend to believe it myself. I tried out the process that evening on the family when I joined them for supper. It went surprisingly well. When I informed the Queen's Grove folk they immediately started to give me lists of things they wanted from America. In the end I had a mass of requests which I guessed I might not be able to fulfil; unless it was Canada again? But if it was Canada, why had we been told to bring civilian clothes?

The Wren Officers going with me were Marjorie and Eve. Eve was an attractive married woman whose husband had been missing for four years. By this time she had presumed him dead. She was a very merry widow who had accustomed herself to her situation and did not intend to remain a widow long. We three of us talked gaily about New York even when we were on our own. There was less chance of a slip-up that way.

19.

Eve, Marjorie and I had to report to Southampton to join the SS Franconia. We had our great coats with us, navy issue sweaters, a scarf, warm boots and fur-lined gloves. Where were we going and when would we know? We both opted for Russia, thinking that it would be Moscow, where Churchill had already been to meet Stalin in October. Roosevelt had not been there on that occasion as he had been campaigning for re-election as President for a fourth term.

There was a crowd of people coming on board. The quarters assigned to the Wren officers were unbelievable. It appeared to be a large mess deck into which fifty or more double bunks had been put in, higgledy-piggledy, cheek by jowl. There was about a foot between bunks. Here we were obviously the lowest of the low. Whoever had planned this trip had not had much thought for our comfort on what might be a long voyage.

At sea it was cold and rough in the January weather. In the Bay of Biscay the real trouble began. Everyone became ill. It was a fearsome nightmare. No-one could sleep because of the airless, noisy, confined and disturbed dormitory. With everyone around you being seasick, with the ship constantly creaking and rocking, the smell of vomit and newly painted bulkheads, my memory of it is that most of us wondered how long we could continue to endure it.

Our gallant and tough senior Wren Officer, First Officer Medley came to our rescue. She had to storm the establishment bastions. She had a right royal tussle before she got any concessions but finally she got our quarters reorganised. She discovered that a lot of the top people, particularly the Cabinet Office personnel, had been assigned, or had assigned themselves, large, quite luxurious cabins, many of them restored to peace-time elegance for the voyage. By making herself really unpleasant she managed to get some of the less senior people to double up and free some cabins for us. By this time, a lot of us were so weak from sickness that we could hardly stagger to the loo. The delight at finding ourselves in a cabin for two, with proper beds, a porthole, light and air, cured most of us rapidly.

By that time we had also left the monstrously rough Bay behind us and were approaching the Straits of Gibraltar. Eve and I, who shared a cabin, could hardly believe our luck. The sun had begun to shine, the sea became bluer every day and my sea legs were back. It became just like old times on the Mauretania, except that it was more interesting as we had so many well-known war-time faces on board. We had no duties yet and almost overnight it became a unique kind of cruise, with deck games, parties every night in someone's cabin, delicious food and irresistibly cheap drinks.

The VIP's, Churchill, Eden, Churchill's daughter, Sarah, and his immediate staff were not on board as they would be flying out later. We found out where we were going: to the Crimea. The civilian clothes would be required for passing through Turkish territorial waters. Turkey was still officially neutral and could not permit warships through the Dardanelles. We were not exactly a warship, but it was a moot point. Some genius had worked out a compromise. Turkey was obviously going to have to put its blind eye to the telescope.

In the Mediterranean it turned grey and we seemed to have lost the postcard blue. We were escorted by destroyers as we steamed steadily eastward. There was some chance of a German air or U-boat attack. If the German High Command had got wind of the number of top brass on board the Franconia we should have been a vital target to take out at all costs. However, by January, 1945, Germany was being pressed hard on two fronts and the U-boat and the Luftwaffe no longer had their old power. This was undoubtedly appreciated by those in the know. For most of us, Hitler was still the great evil spider who might launch another secret weapon at us at any moment, which added a certain spice to the voyage.

Among the many VIP's on board was General Sir Hastings Ismay, Secretary to the War Cabinet, known as "Pug" Ismay. This was a perfect name for him as he did have a look of that tough, intelligent dog. Known for his diplomacy and skill at pouring oil on troubled waters he was also a man with a great sense of humour and a lot of charm. He liked playing poker and liar dice. A group of us joined in several games with him after dinner. We had to put in a small ante to make the game more amusing but it was noticeable that General Ismay kept a sharp eye on the player's rank and therefore his or her presumed financial backing, and he would not let anyone lose too much money. We only noticed this after some time because he achieved it so subtly. He would suggest a changeover of players, or a change of game at some point, and the real reason for this was not apparent; we were being watched over by a kindly father figure out to spot trouble before it arose.

We were making for Malta, the George Cross Island, which had survived combined Italian and German air attacks in 1942. The Luftwaffe then had air bases in Crete and North Africa and were able to destroy most convoys attempting to get through with vital supplies. Ships in Valetta harbour were sailed to safety or scuttled. Food became scarce and the population lived underground by day. The memory of their heroic resistance was in our minds and we were about to see the awful destruction for ourselves.

As we approached the famous harbour some of us went up on deck to get a good view. My great grandfather had been the Commander in charge of the guns defending this harbour. I wondered if we should be allowed ashore.

Now we could see the cruel chaos: streets of houses like the bottom half of a jaw bone with most of the teeth knocked out. All round the harbour were derelict and useless ships. What had once been a thriving and beautiful harbour was a tragic mess of twisted metal, deep holes blown in the high surrounding rocks and bits of cranes pitifully appealing to the sky. Across the entrance to the harbour stretched a boom with anti-submarine nets attached. On the port side of this boom was a narrow entrance, free of nets, just about the width of the ship. It suddenly seemed very clear that we were moving through the water much too rapidly to steer towards that gap. The engines were stopped but we had weigh on, a powerful forward compulsion. It was obvious to all of us standing there that we were heading straight for the nets.

At that precise moment the Senior Naval officer on board appeared on our deck, which was just below the bridge. He was

110

not in charge of the ship which, being a merchant ship, was commanded by its regular peacetime captain in the Merchant Navy. The Senior Naval Officer was frantic, marching up and down, going mad with frustration, muttering and cursing the captain.

'The idiot! What does he think he's doing? He's going to foul the net.'

We all of us stood transfixed as the great bows moved slowly but inexorably towards that sinister net. Even if the order "Full astern" was given now it would be too late. We seemed to be gliding silently ahead as if we were under a spell. What at first had seemed absurd, then possible became, no shadow of doubt, certain. Bad seamanship, or bad luck was taking us straight to disaster.

We hit the net. We fouled our propellers. Instead of a quick in and out, as had been planned, we were delayed for about thirty-six hours while the net was extracted and the propellers repaired. We felt extremely sorry for the Captain. The Harbour Master of Valetta cannot have been very pleased either, since his anti-submarine net was now useless. However his shipyard workers managed to repair the Franconia in record time, working day and night. It meant, too, that we had leave to go ashore. But we wondered if the date of the Conference would have to be put forward with all the colossal reorganisation that would require.

Ashore some of us climbed up to the Gardens which overlook the harbour, possibly once the most dramatic and beautiful harbour in the world. We idled like tourists in the narrow streets, admiring the lace and watching the lacemakers. Their fingers flew with such speed that the delicate clicking of the bobbins was like the sound of a hundred tiny feet on the hollow lace pillows. They hardly seemed to stop even to move the necessary pins as the stitches were formed. The women all wore black and chatted in Maltese, a language believed to contain traces of Phoenician from the occupation of the island by the Phoenicians in the 8th or 9th century BC. They only glanced at us, they were used to uniforms. I admired one old lady's skill but she gap-toothily indicated that she did not understand a word I said.

I had heard tales about the Opera House. My grandmother had been engaged to an Irish cavalry officer who rode his horse up the steps of the entrance and scandalised everyone. Whether it was because of this episode or not he got packed off to India and their engagement was broken off. My grandmother talked about him with a sparkle in her eye; I think she rather regretted her Irishman.

The steps were there, but where was the Opera House? Beyond the high flight of steps, which must have taken a very good horse to mount, there was just a broken ruin.

The ship repaired and at sea again it seemed that we would be able to catch up the lost time, provided there were no other hazards. We were back to the deck games, reading, gossiping and going to more parties. The leading ladies at these functions were the civilians from the Cabinet Office, high-powered, most of them "well-connected" and friendly, although one or two of them tended to be slightly condescending to the women in uniform.

We sailed past the island of Lampedusa. It looked beautiful with the sun shining full on it but a few days later there was a tragic accident. One of the planes carrying personnel to attend the Conference crashed there with the loss of everyone on board.

As we approached Turkish Territorial Waters everyone was ordered into civilian clothes. Instead of an allied ship on its way to discuss the defeat of Germany we had changed overnight into just a merchant ship on a holiday cruise. This had a very curious effect. No longer were we able to read the signs of rank. Merchant Navy ratings, especially those from the engine room, appeared in very smart suits, seizing the chance to take the air on the main deck and mingle with the motley crowd. Every man and woman had their own interpretation of the order to bring civilian clothes and suddenly there were many varied, and some startling, expressions of personality to be seen. The shoulder tabs, caps, sleeves, all insignia of rank had gone, leaving each person somewhat deprived and startlingly "normal". It had its

112

funny side. It was easy to spot many of the really top people because they had brought battered tweed jackets, unpressed trousers and rather soiled but rafish fishing hats which obviously were their preferred "civvy street" wear. We had walked through into Alice's looking-glass land.

Knowing that at some time we should pass near the coast where Troy might have been sited, I went to the Chart Room to see if it was marked. It wasn't. Very little archaeological work had been done on the site at that date. What surprised me was that nobody else on that entire ship appeared to be interested. Perhaps some were but I didn't meet them. It was long before Sir Mortimer Wheeler began the popular interest in "digs". Besotted with tales of the Wooden Horse and the brave but possibly tiresome Achilles, I stared at the opposite shore on the starboard side completely on my own. I was staring at a featureless coastline but it was easy to fill it with Greek ships, tents and shining shields and swords.

We sailed through the Dardenelles and into the Sea of Marmara. When we reached Istanbul, everybody rushed to the port side, almost causing the huge ship to list. There was the great city looking unbelievably exciting, the sun shining full on a huge dome on a hill, squared by its attendant minarets. The dome had a commanding position and was of such sparkling reflected light that, among all the domes and towers of the city, it demanded our attention. It was tantalising that we had to sail by all that glory.

We had reached a point where the Sea of Marmara meets the Bosphorus. Now we were turning to enter the narrow straits of the Bosphorus, only about a mile wide, with the shores on either side standing high out of the water, mostly wooded, making a green backcloth for the few buildings, palaces, mosques and the occasional village. We wanted to see both banks at once and tore from side to side. Military experts were on the Asian side, pointing out Scutari and refighting the Crimean war. On the European side, after a short distance from the Golden Horn, there was the most exquisite tiny white mosque low on the water's edge. It stood quite by itself, surrounded by trees. The sunlight and the reflection of the

113

dancing light from the water floodlit the mosque like a small, intensely white ivory chess piece. Nobody could tell me its name. Whoever the architect was, he knew that it was just that spot where his mosque would dramatise the already beautiful waterway.

After the Bosphorus we entered the Black Sea. George Sandys wrote in 1610 that the Black Sea . . . "so named of its blacke effects. This sea is less salt than others, and much annoyed with ice in winter."

The "annoying" ice, carried in bad winters from the Black Sea down the Bosphorus, has caused damage to the old walls of Istanbul; it has even been strong enough on occasion to allow people to walk across the pack ice from one side of the Bosphorus to the other.

As we sailed north the weather changed and became colder. Once north of the mouth of the Danube we left the early spring behind and returned to winter. We put our uniforms back on again and normal service life and heirarchy was resumed.

20.

Our destination was Sevastopol.   Here the Franconia would dock and remain as the Communications Centre while the Conference itself would take place some miles away by road at Alupka and Yalta.   A vast amount of stores and equipment had to be landed and driven to the palace assigned to the British Delegation.   Everyone put the delights of the holiday-like cruise behind them and got up on their toes.   Because of our delay in Malta we now had quite a tight schedule to get everything ready on time.

We approached the Russian coast.   It looked very cold, grey and uninviting.   The Crimea was like a foot stuck out into the Black Sea from the vast land mass of the USSR.   Here ahead of us was the great continent of one of our allies.   We stared in silence.   It seemed that the sun had left the world.

We tied up alongside a completely flattened dock.   There was little to be seen except stones and piles of bricks that must once have been the harbour buildings.   We dropped anchor.

Nothing happened.   Eventually several Russian speakers went ashore to find out what was planned.   There was no time to waste.   Where were the promised craft we needed to take our equipment ashore?

The Russians were polite but much regretted that nothing could be done.

Why not?

There were no boats available.   The road to Yalta was blocked with snow.   Quite impassable.   We were informed that we would have to wait for a thaw.

If it hadn't been tragic it was almost laughable, this meeting between East and West.   How could the preparations for a Heads of State Conference be held up waiting for a thaw? The planners of D-Day were flabbergasted and then outraged. What organisation was this?   What were the Russians playing at?   Perhaps they did not want us to land.   The impression given was that they had regretted asking us to come.

Diplomacy was tried again.   One of the translators was Polish.   He said it was like talking to the Great Wall of China.

115

Right, decided our top brass, if the Russians are not going to do anything we handle this ourselves.   Fortunately we had a DUK on board, a useful small craft into which the first contingent of men and stores was loaded.   Watched anxiously by all of us on deck, it made for a flat area on the left of our anchorage with a slight stone slope out of the water.   Would the Russians intervene and try to stop us?   We were, in fact, making an illegal landing on their territory.

'What about the blocked road?' I asked one of the naval officers who seemed to know what was going on.

'We think it's balls,' he said pleasantly.

The first Land Rovers got away, packed with equipment, and they reported that although conditions were a bit icy, the road was perfectly clear.   There was no interference from anyone.   The Russian harbour authorities stood and watched as more and more material was landed on Russian soil.   The officers and men responsible for setting up the British Delegation at Yalta just got on with the job.   The Russians might not have been there at all.   Why did they welcome us like this?   We never discovered.   The most likely explanation was a snarl-up in the chain of command.

Once the *fait accompli* had happened, however, cordial exchanges began to take place.   Perhaps word had seeped through from Moscow to get on with it.   The entire ship's company was invited ashore to visit the devastated city and to attend a special concert.   At last things were moving.

A small group of us went ashore.   It was a strange sensation setting foot in an alien land about which few of us knew very much.   It could have been the planet Uranus.   It was first, and above every other sensation, the most depressing sight I had ever seen.   Hitler's mark was here.   He had begun the invasion of the USSR in June, 1941 and attacked Sevastopol in October.   By May 1942 the Germans had captured the whole of the Crimea except Sevastopol.   The city held out for two hundred and fifty days, falling at last in July 1942.   This heroic defence had been vital in holding up the German attack on Leningrad as it meant that Hitler could not move his Eleventh Army until the city capitulated.   The toll was terrible.

Wherever one looked was devastation, an entire city bombed and blasted into a heap of rubble. As we drove towards what had been the centre there were a few little tin pipes, makeshift chimneys, sticking out of the piles of bricks and stones and smoking away. These were the only evidence that there was still a room intact, or shelter of some sort under the rubble, where someone was able to make a fire and cook.

We drove to what had once been the Cathedral of Sevastopol. Above ground was an untouched ruin, a builder's yard of split masonry with hardly a broken column upright among the bricks and dust. We followed our Russian guide to the Crypt below ground which had by a miracle survived.

Above ground all was desolation but in the Crypt we found a huge crowd of worshippers. A service was in progress. So many people were packed into the dark interior, all standing, that it seemed we could only take a quick look from the doorway. But somehow the congregation squeezed together and several nearest to us beckoned us to come in. There was a strong smell, a mixture of candlewax, incense and a strange exotic perfume.

A priest in magnificent embroidered robes of gold on white was chanting, the congregation responding with a muttered fervour that was powerful, echoing and re-echoing from the surrounding cellar-like chapels. We had been told that there was no longer any religion in the USSR. What was this? The icons on every wall, the gold and mosaic decoration, the high and hysterical-sounding chants and answering echoes seemed to come close to the mysteries of early Christianity, long lost by the comfortable English Established Church. The dark crypt made it very easy to imagine the stress and devotion of those early Christians who had also worshipped underground.

We looked around discreetly at the congregation: all of them were old, there was not a young person there. We did not want to appear to be staring, but as we looked there were eyes everywhere, chanting and staring at us, staring at uniforms of a quality they had obviously not seen for a long time, at women with make-up, all of us fair-skinned and well-fed. What did they think of us? The many eyes were dull but not hostile. Way was made for us to go to the front of the congregation.

117

Ahead of us were more ikons, more Byzantine faces staring black-eyed into space, probably centuries old.

After a little time we felt alien and embarrassed. We could not join in the responses nor could we share the memory of the horror of this besieged city or their bereavement. We signalled to each other that it was time to leave. Avoiding the eyes, we tiptoed out again, the more religious, or more polite among us, stopping to genuflect towards the main altar in respect.

Outside in the cold fresh air, one of our group confessed that if he had not got out then he would have passed out.

Outside, in areas which had been cleared and were once streets, we saw old women who were almost square with layers of clothing, skirt over skirt and shawl over shawl. There were very few men and again not one single young person. By the side of the road there was an old man with a cart which had a very large glass jar on it, filled with what looked like water reddened with cochineal. Was it a fruit drink of some sort? People occasionally stopped and bought a cupful, which they drank on the spot, handing the cup back for the next drinker.

'How much would you drink some of that for?' asked one of our party.

'I wouldn't if I were you, not for any money, unless you want to die of poisoning.'

We were smug and superior but, without wanting to show it, extremely shocked by the drabness, the poverty, the lack of anything beautiful anywhere. The only evidence of an attempt to build anything were huge bill boards to take the ubiquitous posters of Stalin and Lenin. I thought they ought to have used the time and the wood to try and put up a few huts for accommodation.

The same thought occurred when we were taken to a hill to see the monument, built to commemorate the siege and the dead. A sad and ugly grey statue. Food, shelter and material goods were what was needed here, but how to get them? We felt angry, no-one appeared to be organising anything while the population who remained of this once great city were desperately trying to survive. Were those two ugly faces on the posters and a grey statue any sort of sop to this misery?

Perhaps we were wrong. At least they had a theatre. This was a large, cheerless drill hall type building with a stage. That evening, a large group of us went ashore again for the concert. Our guide was a frightened little lady who said she was a teacher. She must have been ordered to take charge of us, rather unexpectedly we guessed, because she was possibly the only person in Sevastopol who could speak a little English. At the entrance she ordered us to split up and told each of us to sit next to a Russian. This was a good idea but it was not introduced in quite the right way; her crisp order, as if addressing the first form, did not appeal to the majority of the British contingent, most of them rather large and important high-ranking officers, not used to taking even suggestions from "foreigners" and only the stronger characters took up the challenge. I am sorry to say that the rest of us thought it a stupid idea, since we would not be able to exchange a single word with our unknown neighbour. We much preferred to enjoy the evening's entertainment sitting with our friends. We rudely, but perhaps understandably, ignored her shouts and sat with chosen companions.

Although Russia had been our ally since 1941, there were many among us who had a horror of Communism. All too clear were the memories of Ekaterinburg and the murder of the Russian royal family. It was easy to imagine these ill-dressed, rough-looking folk in the role of the Bolshevik peasants who had hacked people to death. Thoughts of their gallant defence of their city were not uppermost in a lot of our minds, I suspect. Several of the British high-ups were behaving with a disdain that was reminiscent of the English aristocrat's view of the French revolutionary rabble of the 1790's.

The red curtain went up to frenzied applause from the Russians and polite clapping from us as a team of Russian dancers and singers came on to the stage. The Company had come from Moscow and the evening had, of course, been specially arranged in honour of the Conference. It was likely that for the Russian members of the audience it was their first chance to see the Company since the siege.

Before each item the Russian Master of Ceremonies came to the front of the stage and gave an explanation of what we were

119

about to see. We guessed from the length of his talk that he was also giving a historical explanation of the piece and details of who would be performing. We eagerly awaited the translation.

Our translator was none other than the Russian teacher who had brought us to the theatre. She appeared on stage rather suddenly, as if she had been given a push from behind the curtain and she seemed more terrified than she had been before. She came to the front of the stage, wild-eyed, staring at the ceiling and called out in a high-pitched voice:

'A Russian song,' or next item:

'Cossack dance,' and beat a hasty retreat backstage. Her English was obviously not quite up to this and I don't suppose she had been given any warning of this terrible task or given the text of what she would have to translate beforehand. We wondered at the contrast between this ad-hoc arrangement and the astonishing professional skill of the performers.

Our experience that evening was never to be forgotten. The energy, speed and strength of the male dancers in their Cossack uniforms, leaping and crouching, filling the stage with thunderous noise, the very loud and exciting music that punctuated their movements with absolute precision, produced an hypnotic excitement. In contrast to the greyness and hopelessness outside, inside it was difficult to breathe with the tension and thrill and the complete ecstasy of the Russian audience. The magnificent singing of the now famous Russian songs, then unheard by most of us, lifted us to the skies.

Top of the bill was the sword dance, where huge swords crashed and clashed, sparks flying into the air, when a mistake would seem to mean a severed arm or ear; music, clashes, squats, twirls, thrusts, clangs and lunges built into such a crescendo of controlled energy that the only possible release seemed to be for the ceiling to fall in.

Now every single person in that audience joined in the cheering and the tremendous applause. If only we had been able to stay behind after the show and meet and attempt to communicate with the Russian half of the audience, sympathy would have flowed. It was late and we were all due back on board the ship. It was a lost opportunity.

21.

Work began in earnest. We operated in three watches, four hours on duty and eight off, which gave one time to sleep and eat and not much more. The atmosphere below deck, in the Communcations area we had been allotted, was crowded and claustrophobic. It was also quite exhausting as we all of us worked flat out during the time on watch. The signals coming in were unrelenting. They were from all over the world, a lot of them Top Secret and many addressed to the Prime Minister or Anthony Eden and the Heads of the three services. Going out was a stream of replies, commands and routine orders. General Eisenhower was always known as Ike in signals and Churchill had the nom-de-plume of Colonel Warden.

We had to work fast. It was alarming. We dared not make a careless or tired slip working on this vital material, which enabled the politicians and the service leaders to keep in hourly touch with the war fronts, the troop movements, gains and losses, as well as a hundred other details of government considered important enough to refer to the Prime Minister or the Foreign Secretary. It was awe-inspiring, too; here we innocents were, in the middle of great events. What we fortunately could not know were the unhappy consequences of some of the decisions taken at the Conference, nor did we hear more than a rumour of the weakness of the already sick President Roosevelt, who believed that he could charm Stalin off his perch as he had charmed and influenced so many of his countrymen. We were, unknowingly, the pall bearers at a Polish funeral. We thought we were the hand maidens of history in the making, which in a humble sense we were, but we imagined that after the total defeat of Germany the Allies would organise a better world for everyone. This was their unequalled opportunity.

The signals themselves were maddening to anyone who was an honorary member of the N-Parker family who wanted to know the next move, and what happened afterwards, as they were just bits of a very complex tapestry. There was just time to be alerted and interested and then the story vanished into the darkness of other people's in-trays. Anyway, it was not our business to piece the story together, just get on with decyphering the next signal or work through a huge batch of signals on the teleprinter.

Very infuriating were the eager senior officers who liked to come round and peer over one's shoulders as we were decoding a signal, reading it as it came into plain language.   It was difficult to concentrate and easy to make an error.   One tiresome man was always doing this.   In fury I swung round in my chair and sent him a basilisk stare in peevish bad humour, but he was quite blind to my unspoken message, saying crossly 'Well, get on, get on . . .'

Churchill's own messages were normally drafted by his staff but there was one short signal from the great man himself with his initials thinly pencilled at the bottom: WSC.   We were all of us his entirely devoted fans, this great humourist who had led us almost to victory.   ALL of us would have liked to own that tiny scribble.

The Senior Wren Officer of the watch cut the initials off the bottom of the signal and wrote all our names on torn off scraps of a signal pad, folded them and put them in a tricorne.

There was a lull in the work while the hat was carefully shaken.   I felt I couldn't bear to witness the draw and went back to the next signal on that never-ending pile.   I did not hear the result as the noise of the typewriters, teleprinters and people was too great, but there was a tap on my shoulder.   My name had been drawn out of the hat.   The Head of the Watch handed me the scrap of precious paper.

Churchill and his daughter, Anthony Eden, Field-Marshal Sir Alan Brooke, Field-Marshal Sir Harold Alexander and General Gort had met the President, Averell Harriman and staff in Malta for pre-conference talks.   They had then flown to Saki airfield in the Crimea and had had an eight hour car journey to Yalta.

The British, American and Russian delegations occupied three different palaces.   The Soviet Delegation was housed at Koreiz, the estate of Prince Uzupov, who is believed to have assassinated Rasputin.   The American Delegation was in the Summer Palace of Tsar Nicholas II, the Palace of Livadia, presented to the Romanovs by Count Potocki, who had collected rare plants and trees for the parks and gardens. The last Tsar had lived on the first floor and had a number of bedrooms; he would sleep in a different bedroom every night for fear of assassination, sometimes even changing his room during the night. It seemed rather a restless business being a Tsar. Roosevelt's private dining-room had been the Tsar's billiard room. The second floor had been used by the Tsarina and her four daughters. We were told that General Marshall was occupying the Imperial bedroom and Admiral King the Tsarina's boudoir, outside which was the private staircase said to have been used by Rasputin.

The British Delegation was housed in the Château built for Prince Vorontsov in 1837 at a cost of three million roubles from the plans of an English architect called Blore. The Château was surrounded by a magnificent park filled with cypresses and rare sub-tropical plants. Two of the cypress trees in the courtyard had been planted by Potemkin. Prince Vorontsov had been the Russian ambassador to Britain, which was perhaps why it had been chosen to house the British Delegation. The Germans had used it as their headquarters and we heard that it was less damaged than other buildings roundabout.

Eve had been chosen to be the Wren Officer in charge of a small contingent of Wrens at the Château. We were all envious when she went off in one of the Navy cars, but we soon heard that she had problems. Our Russian hosts informed Eve that on no account could she lock up our signal books. They tried, rather naively, to trick her into letting them put the books "in a safe place" overnight. She was not having any of that, these books were very secret, and she arranged a system so that they were always in somebody's charge day and night. Being a little less naive nowadays, I presume that Russian Intelligence may have already cracked our codes. There were probably not the advanced devices which have made keeping secrets, or getting hold of them, such an ultra scientific business, but educated now by Le Carré I realise we were naive indeed. It would be interesting to read the Russian Intelligence archives on Yalta.

On the third day of the Conference, one of the British naval officers had to go to the Vorontsov villa. He asked two of us coming sleepily off night watch if we would like to go with him. *Would we?* It meant leaving at once, no time to have breakfast. It was too exciting to think of sleep. We both grabbed cups of strong coffee, got our greatcoats and ran.

It was early morning. The sun was barely up but the snow which had lain around since our arrival had almost disappeared. The hitherto black, sad landscape had a new look about it, as though spring might even come here. It was delightful to be on shore. We clambered into the truck, greeted our Marine driver and felt like a couple of ten-year-olds let out of school.

The road was narrow but there were no other cars. It would take us about two and a half hours to get there. We drove towards the south east and passed on our right the English cemetery. Then the road became very winding although we seemed to go at breakneck speed between steep walls of rock. Our driver was very pleased to be at the wheel and slapped into his gear changes and jerked the truck round bends with inches to spare. We were much too exhilerated to care about anything and swung from side to side merrily with the swing of the truck.

All the time we were gradually going uphill, through villages which had once been lived in by Greeks and then by Tartars, through woods of oak and beech. We were climbing higher and higher, and the sun began to shine more warmly as we emerged each time from the shadows of the trees. Then suddenly, ahead of us, appeared to be a wall of rock with no visible way around it. At the very summit of the road we saw a gateway ahead. This was the Baidar Gate which had been blasted through the limestone rock in 1848. We drove through and then had to stop the truck on the other side in complete amazement. Below us was a different world. It was a Mediterranean landscape, descending gradually, not unlike the Grande Corniche but not yet spoilt by houses and apartment blocks cramming the view, but lonely, romantic, beautiful. There were pines, cypresses, fig-trees. Nobody seemed to be alive in this landscape except us. The road we could see zig-zagged down from this watershed and just visible in the far distance the sea sparkled. It was not the wintry-looking sea we had left behind in Sevastopol but a glimpse of sunlight dancing on blue water. Now we could understand why this part of the Crimea was the great Russian holiday resort from the days of the Tsar to the "good" communists who were awarded a holiday in one of the remodelled villas.

As we drove down into the valley we passed vineyards, once part of great estates. The ghosts of the Russian past were here. Cakhtchi Sarai, a name which fills the mouth with the pleasure of saying it (like Nevsky Prospekt and Tsarkoe Selo), was the Palace of Gardens where the ruling Khans had lived from the later fifteen hundreds until 1783, when the Russians forced the last Khan to abdicate and it became another Russian province. Most of the Tartars emigrated to Turkey and those who remained became peasants who worked in the fields for their new masters.

A great many of the villas had been destroyed by the German army in 1941. We passed the small villa above Yalta where Chekhov spent the last four years of his life. This had been preserved from destruction - was this thanks to a well-read German officer we wondered? (From later reading I understand this is exactly what occurred.) Chekhov's sister, we were told, was still alive and she had managed to save the contents of the house and it was now a museum.

We drove past the Palace of Livadia. We had heard that the architect had had to make alterations to suit the whims of the Tsar. As he did not approve of these changes to his plans, he got his revenge by using lionhead caricatures of the Tsar as arm rests on two marble benches outside the main door. Apparently the similarity to the Tsar became striking when the cap he used to wear was put on top of the lion's head.

The Imperial family used to come to Sevastopol by train and then continue by yacht to Livadia. But they only stayed in the Palace four times. After the revolution, the Palace became a rest home for tubercular patients. The German High Command had commandeered and ruthlessly looted the contents. Apparently the only items left behind were two pictures in the room occupied by President Roosevelt.

We drove on through Livadia, passing a Moorish château which had belonged to the Grand Duke Dmitri Constantinovich, a resounding name, and the remains of a Roman fortification. The surrounding countryside was magnificent. We thought then that the whole area merited becoming one of the world's playgrounds. Unfortunately we now appreciate what this means: the invasion of people seeking the sun, followed by concrete, followed by yet more people until only the very old can remember the beauty of the past.

We arrived at the Vorontsov villa. It seemed a huge house with an odd mixture of styles. Sarah Churchill described it as being "like a Scottish baronial hall inside and a Swiss chalet with a mosque attached outside". (From her book "A Thread in the Tapestry".) We had heard from Joan Bright, who as General Ismay's assistant had had the awful responsibility of arranging the rooms for all the high-ups, that the conditions were not ideal: two bathrooms per thirty people. The Russians had done their best but the old villa had not been planned for a modern conference. They had been told that each party would consist of thirty-five people: the actual number was five hundred. It was rumoured that sixteen American colonels were sharing one bedroom.

Stalin had ordered the villas to be brought back to something of their old magnificence for the Conference. Carpets, curtains, furniture, pictures, china and silver from old houses and museums in Moscow and Leningrad had been sent to Yalta. They also brought out of retirement old gentlemen who had been valets, waiters and major domos, who could still remember the old style and the old ways. The Russians had done everything they could to insure the comfort of the visitors and give them a vision of Imperial days. What did bathrooms matter?

We arrived at the front door of the villa. It was opened for us by a stooping gentleman in an old fashioned frock coat who would not have been out of place at the Rostov family home. He went at once to a small cupboard and brought out a clothes brush with which he very quickly and expertly brushed us down in turn, saying "Pozhalysto". We presumed this to be part of

Russian etiquette: did it originate when visitors came in out of the snow? Perhaps we were dusty from the road? I felt we had walked into a play by Chekhov or Turgenev. There was something in the air of that dark hall, the past was breathing audibly here; permeating everywhere was a strong scent, an exotic Eastern mix of spices.

We were shown into a small dining-room and sat down at one of the round tables, quite bare except for a white damask tablecloth. Two members of the delegation came to meet us and sat with us at the table. A waiter, another very old gentleman, brought a glass water bottle and some glasses. He poured some for each of us and I gratefully took a thirst-quenching mouthful . . . but it was not water but vodka. The sharp sting and surprise of it made my eyes water. The two delegation members who were used to the innocuous-looking bottles laughed. After our night watch and long drive it woke us up splendidly. There were several toasts: "Schvaszistrovia!" It was not polite to leave a drop in the glass.

We were taken next on a tour of the building. Everything was quiet. The work that morning was going on at the Palace of Livadia and most of the Big Wiggery were safely out of the way. We were free to wander, more or less, where our hosts led us.

First we went to see Churchill's movable Map Room, under the care of a naval Commander and his personal assistant, an attractive redhead called Diana, both of whom we had got to know on board the Franconia. The Map Room had four walls and a door and was completely private. It could be packed up and moved to wherever the Prime Minister was and it followed him to all the Conferences. Here it was set up in the middle of the villa library. We were invited inside and there, on each of the four walls, were the maps of the campaigns at present in progress in the various war zones, with up-to-the-minute dispositions of every unit marked with coloured flags. Churchill's round leather chair was in the centre. Here he could sit and swing round to view any battle area he wished. I remember that the advance towards Germany seemed heartening, although the first crossing of the Rhine would not take place until March. We took turns in sitting in the famous chair.

The Commander and Diana were amusing and full of stories of their great master and the Prime Minister's valet, Sawyers. Sawyers, the source of many jokes, had been knocked for six by the vodka but still managed to preserve his rather acid and unvalet-like attitude to Churchill, whom he cheeked and cossetted in the manner of a favourite Court Jester.

We were taken to a dark dining-room where the three Heads of State, Churchill, Roosevelt and Stalin would be dining that evening. The large round table was already laid for dinner; set near a window, it was laid for ten people and was a fine display of beautiful glass, silver and damask. The Tsar himself would not have found much amiss, I thought.

22.

On board the Franconia the following day, Marjorie, one of the three Wren officers from Flag Officer Submarines, developed violent toothache. The medical officer on board was a doctor not a dentist. Marjorie had fearful thoughts of being put ashore to try and find a Russian dentist, if one existed in that wilderness of a city, but soon the pain became so acute that she ceased to think of anything except a means to end it.

Moored some distance from us was the American aircraft carrier, USS Catoctin, which had brought Roosevelt's conference personnel to Sevastopol. A signal was sent by our doctor asking if by chance the Catoctin had a dentist on board. Back came a signal immediately saying that they had and that he would be delighted to offer his services to any British personnel in need of dental care. Marjorie was told to stand by while one of the cutters was lowered to take her over to the Catoctin. With only a foothold on reality due to lack of sleep, I went with her as comforter stroke chaperone. My official role was the latter.

We sped across the harbour in fine style. The water looked cold and grey today and much too close to us; we had got used to seeing it from the superior height of the decks of the Franconia. It was also windy and quite rough; it was not a day to fall in and have to be hauled out. We both grabbed the rating's proferred helping hand very firmly until we had got our feet safely on to the Catoctin's welcoming and wide ladder.

To our amazement and slight embarrassment it was a proper welcome. We were piped aboard and it appeared that half the ship's company were peering from all vantage points to get a look at us. The word had got round that *females* were coming aboard.

Two officers had been detailed to meet us. We were taken to a wide elevator which sped us to a different deck; it was like being in a skyscraper's elevator with the same efficient noises of swishes, clicks and smoothly-opening doors. The green-painted dental surgery was complete with more up-to-date-looking equipment than either of us had seen before. The young dental surgeon was from a Southern state, we guessed, from his honeyed sleepy accent.   He seemed nervous at having to cope with a female patient.

'My assistant is ashore so I will have to ask you to help me with the X-Ray,' he said to me.   With relief I found I had only to press a button.   Marjorie was in such pain that she just looked as if she would pass out if something wasn't done quickly.   The dentist manoeuvred the X-Ray plate into position, gave the signal and I pressed.   Then he disappeared for a long time to develop the print.

He arrived back and confessed sadly that his assistant usually did this job and that he was out of practice and had made a hash of it.   He would have to take a second X-Ray.   This time it worked and it was clear that Marjorie had an abcess.

Whatever he did next was very efficient as her pain subsided.   She slid off the bier-like movable chair so relieved that she began to take in her surroundings and actually talk instead of holding her cheek and making sad grunts.

We were taken to the wardroom for a very delicious cup of coffee.   We were also given a copy of the ship's newspaper, full of funny stories and cartoons - one was of a very drunken rating being brought back on board by two shipmates;   as well as the usual stars above his head were the hammer and sickle.   The caption was "We let him sniff a vodka bottle, sir".   The newsheet was marked "This issue cannot be sent home".

As it was Sunday we were also given a printed sheet of the Order of Worship that day, February 11, 1945, taken by the Chaplain, John B. Nance and including an organ prelude.   The entire ship seemed to us like a giant luxury hotel, although from later reading of contributions in the news-sheet one could guess that that might not be quite how the ship's company would describe it.

We thanked our charming Southerner and said goodbye to the officers who had treated us like visiting royalty, very reluctantly on my part as I was enjoying myself.   Marjorie, who was rather drugged from the anaesthetic, was thankful to be off. We returned to our waiting cutter.   Back in the Franconia Marjorie went straight to bed and I went off to the bar to tell of our adventure to an envious group.   But the short episode had made us all realise what could happen so many miles from home. It was comforting to think of that large grey sea monster at anchor near us, so well-equipped and so kindly disposed.

The following afternoon one of the diplomatic staff in a fuss and flurry asked if I would help him out of a small crisis. He had a Russian General with him but had to attend a meeting. Would I please look after the General for ten or fifteen minutes while he organised something.

We shook hands and I gestured to the General to sit down in one of the deep armchairs in the state-room on the main deck. Having sat down we stared at each other. He looked severe and unhappy. We had been given on arrival in Sevastopol a list of useful words in Russian but (1) we had not had much time to get them by heart and (2) the words chosen were not really much help when it came to trying to ask questions and understand the answers. Here was a problem since the General spoke not one word of English. These idiotic exchanged stares could not go on for ten minutes.

The only hope was to devise an English lesson, my first attempt at the "Direct Method". Pointing to his row upon row of medals I said 'Medals?' This was a mistake as he began to point them out individually (I think) and then told me what he had got them for (I presume); but at least it took up some of the time.

With that warning, I tapped the low table in front of us and said firmly 'Table, this is a table. What is it in Russian?'

He was worried by this. I could have been saying "wood", "it's too small", "put your feet on it", or "shall we order a drink?"

'TABLE. This is a table.'

Pointing to a chair *'This* is a CHAIR; in Russian . . .?'

Light dawned. He responded with a rolling sort of gobble. I tried to say it. It sounded like "I love you" in Russian, which was the one phrase we all of us *had* learnt, bandied about like mad by the officers of the British Delegation. The General looked much too senior to be saying that. More smiles.

'Now you say Table, Chair,' pointing at them. 'Very good.' He was much quicker than I was. 'Now WINDOW . . .

131

I mean PORTHOLE. (Oh dear, always prepare your lesson carefully beforehand.) This produced a broad smile. "Hole" seemed to be a pleasing noise to him and he said "Hole, hole," to himself happily for a few seconds. Never mind, we were getting somewhere. I did my best with the Russian words he produced but as soon as I had repeated them I forgot them. He was warming to the task. I got the Russian for EYES, NOSE, MOUTH, EARS and what could have been NICE WHITE TEETH in a flurry of sound and gesture. (Or he could have been saying the equivalent of 'See no evil, hear no evil . . .) This was exhausting.

The diplomat hurried in to take him back. 'Thank you so much for amusing him,' he said to me. 'Sorry to have been so long.' Then he said something to the General in very fluent-sounding Russian. I boldly rolled out 'Do svidanye' and was surprised by the look of pleasure that crossed the General's face as we shook hands. He said it too, and it sounded almost the same as my rendering. There was a feeling of warmth; we had changed the scene and parted friends.

On February 13th the official communiqué was issued in London by the British Official Wireless Press, and included the phrase "British representatives have brought from Yalta vivid impressions of Russian friendship and particularly Russia's determination to maintain close collaboration between the two countries after the war". At the time we did not question the sincerity of the statement. Now less naive, we know it was the usual diplomatic language which covers half-truths, wishful thinking and sometimes downright lies. The communiqué ended "The Conference will henceforth be known as the CRIMEA CONFERENCE. Marshal Stalin so christened it, and all concerned were delighted with the aptness of the title." History has chosen to ignore the Marshal.

The BBC Dictation News 0800 GMT on the same day read as follows:

"A communique on the Big Three conference in the Crimea says a joint plan has been drawn up for the defeat of Germany and for enforcing unconditional surrender. The three powers will each control part of Germany and a commission consisting of the three Supreme Commanders will sit in Berlin. France is to be invited to share these tasks. German armed forces are to be disbanded, the General Staff broken up, military equipment removed or destroyed, war criminals brought to justice and the Nazi party wiped out. Germany is to pay reparations in kind. The policy for liberated Europe covers emergency relief and the formation of interim governments until free elections can be held. The provisional Polish Government now in Warsaw is to be reformed to include democratic leaders from Poland and from Poles abroad. The Polish frontier is to be the Curzon line, but Poland must receive territory in the North and West. A United Nations Conference will meet in San Francisco on April 25th to draw up a world peace charter."

Churchill at the end of the conference had apparently been unable to make up his mind whether to leave at once, go by air, or go by sea. Then he suddenly decided to come on board the Franconia and "read the newspapers". His valet Sawyers was driven half mad with these changes of plan. Roosevelt had already left and Stalin, as Churchill's daughter wrote "like some genie, just disappeared." A stateroom was given to Churchill and we were told not to tramp about too much on the deck over his head. On the deck below his stateroom, General Ismay passed me in a great hurry, raising his eyebrows and tilting his head to indicate the holy of holies above, saying cheerfully 'He's like a bear with a sore head this morning.'

It was comforting to realise that the "greats" had their problems but were not averse to sharing them. So preferable to the superior tone of secrecy assumed by many officials of lesser standing, who liked to make us feel that we were very small fry.

Both the Prime Minister and Anthony Eden made speeches to the crew on board the Franconia before flying home. We were all given copies. I thought at the time, possibly wrongly, that the PM's speech had been prepared for him but that he had added a phrase or two here and there. It had not got quite the right Churchillian tone - but who were we to expect our great leader's own efforts after such an exhausting and, as it turned out, depressing conference..

PRIME MINISTER'S SPEECH TO THE CREW, ON

BOARD SS FRANCONIA 13TH FEBRUARY, 1945.

"Captain Grattidge, officers and crew of the SS Franconia; it is a great rest and pleasure to me to spend a couple of days on your ship after the hard work we have had to do.   You have made a notable effort to carry out all your tasks, and you have made a vital contribution to the historic conference which has just ended.   You carried here and accommodated signal personnel and communications which have made it possible for me and my advisers to keep in constant touch with the progress of the war and to keep His Majesty's Government in London informed of the progress of the Conference.   You carried here, in addition to a large number of officers and officials who were required for the Conference, motor cars and other transport which enabled the British Delegation who were accommodated in two separate houses to keep in touch with each other and with the American and Russian delegations.   You also carried here all the technical vehicles and equipment which it was necessary to have at the main airfield at which the President and I and nearly all of the high officers of the American and British delegations arrived.   The rapid unloading of this number of vehicles and equipment under the most difficult conditions was a fine achievement and reflects credit on all concerned.   Their rapid reloading will be an arduous task, but I am sure it will be carried through with the same vigour, efficiency and devotion to duty which distinguished it.

"It has, I am afraid, been a great disappointment to you that more use has not been made of the splendid accommodation and conference rooms provided on the ship in case of necessity.   But this necessity, happily, did not arise.   Why did it not arise?   Our Russian friends made such extraordinary exertions that they were able to get their house into good order and we were able to get to our work much quicker on the spot than if we had had to pass to an fro from one place to another.

"The Conference has, as you know, been a great success and I think it has taken measures which will bring peace nearer and also make it stay with us for all time.   You have played a part in this picture and you may one and all be proud of your share in it.

"I wish it had been possible for me to travel some part of the way back with you on your ship, but I have to go on with my duties which are pressing. I have several places to go to and a lot of people to see before I am able to turn my course to Britain again. Thank you all very much for what you have done and for the keenness which you have shown in your work. I have asked the Captain whether he will accede to my request and enable all those who may be so disposed to "splice the main brace" tonight. I trust that this request of mine will be acceded to, and I wish you all the best of good luck, a prosperous voyage home" (what did he mean by "prosperous"?) 'and, when you get back, you will really be able to feel that you have played a part in helping at what may prove to be one of the later milestones in the German war. You have helped in every way and it is my deep regret that I have not been able to profit more of all the services you have been so ready to offer.

"Thank you very much. Goodnight, good luck."

The Foreign Secretary's speech was shorter and seemed obsessed with the "all who sail in her" phrase. We wondered rather rudely at the time if launching ships was Eden's only contact with the sea. But he did say: "Our ability to . . . keep the peace after victory depends on the ability of the Great Three Powers - United States, the British Commonwealth and Empire and Soviet Russia to work together. If they can work together peace is possible, maybe probable, for a generation. If they cannot work together it is hard to see any future but perplexity, suffering and war."

The High-Ups were leaving us, the heavy work was over. It was the time for thanks and congratulations all round. General Ismay visited the Cypher Office and thanked everyone on duty personally and asked for his message to be passed on to the rest of the staff saying that throughout the Conference "there had been complete confidence in your efficiency and accuracy". It was nice to relax and get some praise but we wondered what would have happened if we had not all striven on the top line for efficiency and accuracy. It had been hard work but who would not have dug out in such a situation. We were into the reaction phase.

23.

The return to normality, the usual routine of being on watch at FOS, could have been an anti-climax.   It wasn't because the very fact of having been to Yalta had given us a curious status which we had fun exploiting to the full.

'Tell us what happened?'

'You're so lucky.   I'd have given anything to be there.'

'What was Stalin *really* like'

'Did you meet Churchill?'

The fact that we didn't see, let alone meet, any of the three Great Men, didn't seem to matter.   We had tales to tell and we were firmly installed in the chimney corner and commanded silence.   Even the more senior officers at Northways behaved in a slightly different way towards us.   A little reflected glory is very helpful and we all three grew more confidant in the process. But there were three of us, watching each other's performance as it were, which meant that any real swelling of heads was avoided.   No exaggerations or half truths were permitted. However the chance of being chosen to go to Yalta, which was sheer luck, made me feel more like a responsible adult.   It was a bit like being Alice on the chessboard - I had somehow managed to move on to the next square.

My name had been put forward to do a Signal Course.   To become a Signal Officer would mean taking on a lot more responsibility.   If one passed the course it might also mean, in time, becoming a Second Officer - two blue stripes on the arm and shoulder tabs - and slightly more pay.   Nervous excitement took hold of me again.   Rushing home to give the family the news, my father, who had been a Signal Officer in the First World War, told me that I would probably have to pass an exam in the Morse Code.   This was a sobering thought.   I remembered Nobby Clark, the Senior Wireless Officer on Mauretania, taking down the dots and dashes with insouciance and making immediate sense of a stream of sounds.   I could never . . .

On my pre-course leave, my father set about teaching me. I had to learn a group of dots and dashes every day and he tested me with a knife as the "key", holding the handle flat on the table with one hand and making the long dashes and sharper dots by depressing the blade of the knife with his other hand.   Lunches and dinners became a series of interesting messages which drove everyone else swiftly from the table.

The course took place at the Signal School at Leydene, near Petersfield in Hampshire.   On arrival we were divided into two groups, one being housed in a large requisitioned house near Alton, called Basing Park, the other in the Signal School itself. In the middle of the course the two groups were to change over. Our group drew Basing Park for the first half.

At the beginning we felt rather out of things.   Basing Park was a dark house with too many trees obscuring the light.   We all felt that the fun and excitement was at the Signal School itself.   In the end, however, we were glad it was this way round as we had the best of the course to come and were on the spot for the splendid passing-out party.

Leydene House is an Edwardian mansion which had once belonged to Beatrice Lillie, Lady Peel.   I believe she still owned it at that period of the war but had "lent" it to the Royal Navy, probably a polite way of saying it had been requisitioned.   Until a few years' ago it continued to be HM Signal School, the training establishment for all the Navy's Signal Officers, male and female.   Its watchword was the Drake dictum that the officers should haul and draw with their men, ie: as a signal officer you had to know the entire job from top to bottom, inside out, from the humblest task to the most complex.   Lord Louis Mountbatten was one, if not *the* one who had set about furthering this tradition.   It was Lord Louis who had written a handbook ("The User's Guide to Wireless Equipment") and invented various devices which were adopted by the Navy.   He had lectured at the peace-time Signal School in Portsmouth, had been Fleet Wireless Officer in the Mediterranean before the war and maintained his contact with the Signal School as he rose to higher command.   He wanted signal officers who were not just as efficient as they could humanly be but people who were creative about their jobs and knew how to get the best from their subordinates, as he himself managed to do so supremely well.

137

The team of officers who were in charge of the training were a lively but exigent bunch. Some of the lectures were in panelled classrooms with a raised platform at one end, complete with a lectern. One eccentric character never remained at the lectern for more than his opening words, proceeding to pace backwards and forwards across the platform talking unceasingly and balancing, with his hands in his pockets, on either extreme edge of the platform. He seemed to defy gravity, rocking back on his heels that were already over the edge, but again and again his toes, which must have been magnetic, saved him from tipping over backwards. He certainly kept the class awake but few of us could remember the purport of his lecture as we waited, rivetted, for his fall.

Some of the instruction was outdoors. We strove to learn hand signals with a couple of flags, moving sufficiently smartly to please the instructor, yet not too fast in order to help the group at the other end of the lawn who were trying to read our vital messages. There were lectures on the organisation of a signal office, ashore and afloat, on handling personnel, on communicating in all manner of ways. It was absorbing and exhausting and the thought of the examinations at the end kept us concentrating wonderfully.

My father had been right - the Morse Code was obligatory. A number of the naval officers had no problems since they had been using Morse in their various jobs on board ship. I wondered if I would ever be proficient. An even greater worry was the need to learn how a radio worked.

We were allowed one or two week-end leaves. On one of these I called on my brother John for help; John who had built his own recording machine and for whom I had bought the microphone in New York was just the person to answer my SOS. Sitting with a metaphorical wet towel round my head I tried to grasp his excellent lecture on the hows and whys of radio. Eventually, entirely thanks to John, I became interested and managed not to be scared stupid when confronted by the powerful radio transmitters and receivers at the Signal School. But because it was stuffed into my head for an emergency the facts have gone up the memory spout. There was something called a "super hetrodyne". which had a pleasing sound, but to define it now . . . zilch.

There was no question of relaxing in the evenings. There was a lively social life. There were dances every week at which we did energy tests like "Stripping the Willow" and other reels: the men making loud and exuberant yells from time to time, while we strove to remember the right moves. A certain amount of booze was consumed in the bar, and at dinner, but all of us were careful. We were under observation for leadership behaviour at all hours. Very tiring. Yet "natural" behaviour was required; the staff were with us all the time and joined in all the apres-ski activities - it was no use being shy and frightened or stand-offish, neither could one release too much exuberance. There was no doubt that the extroverts did best, but only the ones who used their brains and imposed a layer of caution over their high spirits. The Navy appreciates daring - but controlled daring - just what is required, one presumed, to captain a ship successfully. As usual, a nice judgement was required.

There were thirty of us, of whom eight were women. The men had arrived from different ships and bases and were all RNVR (Royal Naval Volunteer Reserve). Some of them had come from varied and interesting peacetime jobs. One had been a journalist, another the manager of one of London's largest hotels. In our free time we dashed about the narrow country lanes in cars driven at a speed which did not consider any possibility that another car might be travelling at the same speed but in the opposite direction. One Lieutenant had rows of chickens, a partridge, four pheasants and a blackbird painted on the side of his car, like the airmen with their Nazi "score" painted on the fuselages of their aircraft.

It did not seem strange that we were so few women among these men. Admittedly there were no female instructors, only executive Wren officers who were responsible for our discipline and well-being, one of whom told me my hair was too long. We certainly felt we were in male territory, but I seem to remember that we accepted the situation naturally because of the needs of war. It was quite simple: there were not enough male signal officers to go round, so, we had to train to do the job as best we could. We were, after all, not exactly pioneers. I am sure the first Wren Officers to join the Signal School may have felt they were breaking down traditions, barriers, prejudice and distaste but we did not. By this time, 1945, men who disliked competing with women had had to keep quiet about it. We were neither patronised nor teased.

We used our privileged minority status to the full when it came to the facts we had to learn. We knew about signal offices and how they worked on shore, more or less, but had no notion of what went on at sea. We questioned our fellow officers closely and made copious notes. We went for long walks in two's, asking each other questions, repeating and repeating the items which seemed to us totally obscure, trying to memorise them parrot-fashion. The men were splendidly helpful, telling us generously all they knew but curiously did not seem to want to ask about what *we* knew. When it came to the exams, with questions that drew on our knowledge and experience as well as theirs, the women did rather well, two of them tying for third place out of the entire course.

One of the very pretty girls in the other half of the course had obviously caught the eye of one of the young RN staff. Her name was Catherine and her father was the Master of St. Cross, the beautiful small church in Winchester which since the fourteenth century has served beer and cheese to bona-fide travellers. Towards the end of the course she invited some of us to a dance at her home. Included in the invitation was a young Norwegian officer who had escaped from Norway to join the Allies and who was doing the Signal Course with us. In Norway, we learnt, a vicar is traditionally not given to frivolities of any kind. Monrad, as he was called, who couldn't say his "v's", was amazed to be invited. "A dance?" he asked in amazement, "in a Wicar's house?" We explained to him that all was in order here.

VJ Day - the end of the war in the Far East - came while we were striving to learn the duties of a Signal Officer. This theatre of war had not occupied our daily thoughts in quite the same way as the European War had done. It was as yet too distant, although we duly imagined that on completion of the

140

course we should be sent to one of the bases in the Far East and have our ignorance rapidly dispelled. The order by President Truman to drop the two bombs on Hiroshima and Nagasaki - the horror of this we did not begin to understand - and the subsequent Japanese surrender produced one thought, and one only: thank God it is ALL OVER. No more killing. It had been almost six years of war.

Some of us went up to London to celebrate and we pushed our way through the joyous crowds to join the throng outside Buckingham Palace. We were packed in but there was elbow room and space to change position and walk about. Everyone was talking to everyone else, friend or stranger. The moment we were all waiting for was the opening of the tall double doors in the centre of the balcony. Suddenly the light flashed on the glass as a lackey swung them back. There were the King and Queen waving to the cheering happy crowd. It was a family scene. Those two small figures had shared with everyone the dangers and pains of those years. They were indeed the father and mother of the Nation. We thanked them for their courage throughout the war with burst after burst of roaring hurrahs.

That evening I had to get back to the Signal School on my own. The station at Waterloo was packed to the roof. The train for Petersfield was just about to leave. I ran the length of it, looking frantically for a seat - people were standing shoulder to shoulder, not an inch anywhere. At the far end, beside the engine, was the driver, watching the huge crowd.

'Hello,' he said to me, 'having trouble finding a seat?'

It was the understatement of the year. I told him I wondered if I could sit on the roof.

'Hop in,' he said, indicating his driver's cabin. 'You can help me drive the train.'

I hopped.

The whistle blew, the driver stepped in smartly and slammed the door. He pulled a lever towards him and we were off, steering straight for a fistful of lines at a rather alarming speed. Which line would it be . . . Ooh . . . that one, sharpish to the left. Another spray of lines, off to the right this time. It was getting a bit breakneck.

141

'Do you want to drive her?'

'Yes please.'

'Right.   Sit here' (a sort of lean-against half seat) 'and keep the handle steady.   It's all right, if you let go she slows up - dead man's handle, you see.'   I loosened pressure imperceptibly, yes, good, it did slow up.   But the speed was rather nice.   A definite sense of power.   The only real worry was, again, those different lines stretching ahead and wondering which was the spoke of the fan destined for us.   We talked about the war and all too soon came a station and he took over.   And then, much too soon came Liphook, where I had to get out.

'Thank you for a marvellous journey,' I said.

'Cheerio.'

A lot of people thank the engine driver at the end of a journey and I began to do this, of course keeping an eye open for *my* driver.

'You *drove* the train?' said a number of people at Leydene in disbelief.   'My God, I'm thankful I was not on it.'

24.

At the end of the Signal Course the results of the examinations were read out and we were each told where we would be sent. Catherine and I were appointed to join the Commander in Chief, Naval Forces, Minden, Germany. We had already made friends and were delighted to be sent somewhere together. We were instructed to report to Crosby Hall on the Embankment for the night before flying to Germany.

Catherine, and John the Signal Officer she had met at Leydene, were very much in love and unofficially engaged. When I arrived at the rather gloomy Victorian quarters there was no sign of Catherine. When she did not arrive for dinner I began to wonder what had happened. I was worried for her but very excited for me. Where would I be this time tomorrow? What would Germany be like? Exhilarated and nervous I wished Catherine would turn up. We had to leave very early the next morning - at 5.0 am. I decided it was pointless to wait up for her and went to sleep.

At about four thirty in the morning I was woken by the taffeta rustle of a long skirt. Catherine stood by the bed in an evening dress. She was frantic. John had taken her to Quaglinos for a farewell dinner and her suitcase, all ready for Germany, was stowed in John's MG parked not far from the restaurant. The car had been broken into during the evening and her handbag, suitcase and her uniform had been stolen. All she had were her evening clothes and her greatcoat. It would be out of the question for her to fly that day. We held a whispered conversation.

'What will you do?'

'John is going to help me get a new paybook - it's apparently a terrible sin to lose this - I've got another uniform but it's in Winchester. Thank goodness John is going to tackle their Lordships for me to explain everything. I'll join you as soon as I can.'

'I might as well get up, it's almost time anyway. Take care. See you in Minden.'

And the taffeta rustled out again to the waiting MG.

We had been told that breakfast would be left for us on a shelf in a cupboard. There was a glass of cold milk, a kettle to make tea and a pile of beetroot sandwiches. Obviously the best that Crosby Hall could provide.

It was a very cold and dark morning in January. The river was shrouded in mist. A car was to pick me up and drive me to a building which was part of RAF Transport Command. I was very glad of my greatcoat and stamped my feet to get the circulation going as I waited for the car on the silent Embankment. Once inside the unheated car I huddled deeper inside my coat. The air was very raw. It looked as if it might snow. We drove to a building in Pall Mall.

At least this building was warm. A lot was going on. At intervals a voice on a loudspeaker called out for passengers for Vienna, Paris, Brussels, Copenhagen. It seemed extraordinary that this motley collection of uniforms and plain clothes were about to take the air to these romantic places, forbidden to us for six years. In response to their names, people from different corners got up and made their way to the adjacent room to have their luggage weighed. The atmosphere was brisk and efficient but the comfortable seats almost persuaded me to make up for those lost hours of sleep. It was difficult to stay awake.

At length the call came for the passengers for Buckeburg P1 flight. I staggered with my luggage, nervous that I had brought over the limit. Luckily my effects were weighed in without comment.

By now it seemed to be a little lighter outside. We piled into a large bus and the journey to the airfield lulled most of us back to sleep.

At the airport reception hut were several Naval and Air Force personnel also flying to Germany. I reported Catherine's absence, but due to her fiancé's efficiency they had already had the signal. We hung about waiting, listening to the preparatory roars of an aeroplane wanting to get airborne. We could see a small plane on the tarmac as it gradually became lighter.

'Are we going in that?'

'Yup. As used by His Majesty's paratroopers. Not the most comfortable but it should get us there.' The RAF piece-of-cake nonchalance was meant to be reassuring. This was to be my very first real flight - I had only been up once in a trainer plane, ten shillings for half an hour. I was not nervous, it was too exciting, though the plane did look, especially close to, like one of my brother's models stuck together with glue which normally fell to pieces after a couple of flights.

Inside the plane we took our seats on two long benches, facing inwards. It was hard to see out of the porthole unless you bent backwards and sideways. It had not been designed for relaxed flight as the bar behind one's back was at the most inconvenient angle. Obviously the passengers for whom it was designed were meant to stay alert. On one of the escape hatches opposite me were the printed instructions to troops about to make a parachute jump, with a healthy reminder of when to pull the rip cord. We had been told that in case of necessity our parachutes were stowed under each seat. I felt the bulk of mine with my heel and read the notice carefully. I noticed with secret amusement that the more restless of the passengers were in light blue uniform; dark blue were obviously in happy ignorance.

As we taxied to the waiting position the pilot opened the throttle and put the plane through its paces. The little plane shook with the eagerness to be off and pulled against the restraining grip of the brakes. All seemed to be well. We got the "go" sign and suddenly began to move, racing faster and faster along the tarmac . . . this was amazing, awe-inspiring speed. Then gently the stick went back and those flimsy floppy wings took the air and the ground we could just see was tearing by below us. We were in a new element, the ground had no control over us any more. Flying up and up we could see our hut below was now a miniature lying in the middle of a child's game on a carpet. Then we were away, on course for the North Sea and Germany. From trying to see everything I had got a crick in my neck. Several hours of backaching discomfort lay ahead, eased by friendly shouted exchanges above the roar of the engines and someone's even friendlier flask of brandy being passed round.

145

Minden, once a walled town, was where a battle had been fought in 1759 in the Seven Years' War. On that occasion the British were on the side of Frederick the Great of Prussia against an enemy which included France, Russia, Austria and Sweden. It was now the headquarters of the Senior Naval Officer in Germany.

In the months before D-Day, optimistic preparations had begun for Naval personnel to be sent to Germany to cope with the aftermath of victory. Groups were set up to be sent to the ports: Hamburg, Wilhelmshaven, Kiel, Emden and Cuxhaven. The Naval Parties, each given a number, were to assume that very few buildings would be left standing. It was thought then that the Germans would carry out a scorched earth policy.

When the Allied airborne landings failed and the last German offensive began in December 1944, planning for victory became slightly less urgent and the Naval Parties operation "Eclipse" became temporarily a back number. By February 1945, however, the Allied offensive was reasserting its forward thrust and "Eclipse" filled their Lordships' minds once more. Courses were arranged for officers and men on such subjects as "Booby Traps", "Weapon Training", "Demolition", "Cooking" and "Hygiene". Liaison officers were attached to the 1st and 2nd Army Headquarters to get last minute information on the situation in Germany so that as the ports fell into Allied hands Naval Parties could arrive to take over.

One Commander RN, who had been one of these liaison officers, told us that he wished he could have been attached to the Army for longer. He remembered, rather wistfully, that he would leave his billet in the morning with his belongings all over the place and return at night to discover that an advance had been carried out. All he found was a map reference awaiting him with "On to P.173" or something similar. He duly advanced to P.173 and on arrival he would find the information awaiting him that his new billet was in, say, C Block. Arriving there he would find all his belongings neatly organised. Going in to dinner he would find everything prepared and a Wine Steward asking him what he would like to drink. He said that he never ceased to marvel at the speed and efficiency with which the very swift advance was carried out, and the attention to all the small details that helped to make life easier.

It was a small example of a general change of atmosphere. It now seemed that some of the age-old resentment and rivalry between the Army and the Navy had diminished. It had taken long years of war and drastic changes at the top in Whitehall to bring home to all three services that they were on the same side.

Victory was achieved, the ports were duly taken over and the close co-operation between the Army and Navy continued. When Field Marshal Montgomery set up the headquarters of 21 Army Group, the Senior Naval Officer also moved to Minden.

The Navy had taken over an area and erected a high fence around it. It consisted of several streets of quite large residential houses and in the middle, Dr. Ley's model paper factory. This factory had been designed on ultra modern lines and was considered to be one of the most up-to-date in the country; it was now the Navy's official headquarters.

The Wrens occupied several of the houses. The one I was driven to was on the edge of the perimeter, a pleasant small suburban house. Catherine and I had been assigned a room on the second floor which looked down on to a dusty road with fields beyond. It seemed strange to be looking down into Germany - the compound itself was too British, with its whitened stones, flagstaff, naval personnel going smartly to and fro, to be anything other than a bit of England in a foreign field. But outside our window was another country altogether.

Catherine arrived a week later and we both found that the view from our window, across the wire fence, drew us like a magnet. We had already been told stories of the starvation level of the German people and the utter devastation of the country. We had met members of the Control Commission, put in charge as soon as the military moved on, whose job was to restore order, administer the law, organise emergency housing and food and generally try to alleviate some of the suffering and set the country on the road to being able to govern itself again. Watching the few German civilians who passed along the country road we inevitably had very mixed feelings. We felt pity but also, at first, a sense of triumph: "they" had brought it on

147

themselves, etcetera. But it was one thing to feel fiercely about an enemy from the arms-akimbo position, safely at home, tough and ready for revenge. It was quite different here. A wagon passed with an old driver hunched up, the horse barely plodding. Where was he going to find shelter? Were those battered bits and pieces on the cart his only possessions? And it made me wonder who had been turned out of this very house to accommodate us.

The small bedroom was pleasant. It had two white beds, a white wardrobe, dressing-table and two white chairs. It must have been a nursery. It reminded me of the scene when the curtain goes up in Peter Pan. We put a notice to this effect on our door: "Act I, Scene I, Peter Pan" which we later discovered caused amusement among the top brass who had to carry out inspections.

At the factory we discovered our domain and set to work. Learning the job would be testing, there was so much we did not know. We two were to take over from two Wren officers who were being appointed elsewhere. Our "boss" was Lieutenant Commander Kempson, who made us welcome immediately, introduced us around and quickly made us feel part of his team.

There was a very slight but interesting change which seemed to have taken place in the way in which we were regarded by our fellow officers. Here we were, arriving to take on a particular job for which we had been carefully trained. Unlike being a cypher officer, also trained but one of many, we were now members of a mini corps d'élite. It was assumed that we would take up our appointment, join the team and get on with the job. No-one had to feel too responsible for us; we were responsible for ourselves. Our immediate superiors apparently had faith in us and it was our task to live up to this. We suspected then that it might take a lot of hard work to find the equivalent position in a career outside the Service. We were just beginning to realise that, with the war over, we would have to start thinking of this. Where could we go where we might be regarded as valuable members of a team with the same lack of problems?

That is to say, almost without problems. One morning, the Wardroom President passed on an important message asking the women to be silent at breakfast time; apparently we were spoiling the day's start for several of the crustier members of the top brass. We reacted with astonishment. Totally silent at breakfast was asking too much. However we did make an effort to sit together or with the livelier younger males, leaving the golden-sleeved oldies to their own devices. We made an attempt to tone down the chatter but the general consensus was that they were a lot of miseries best avoided.

Dr. Ley's factory was made of concrete with huge plate glass windows everywhere. The windows were double-glazed, which I had not seen before. In the comfortable wardroom there were radiators the length of each window. After being nearly frozen in the outside winter air it was splendid to sit on one of the sofas up against the radiators and feel the warmth creep through to one's spine. The central heating was a revelation. It was almost worth getting chilled for the pleasure of the caressing heat spreading to my shoulders and down to my fingers and toes. The heat belted out. I am sure the needle must have been on the 80's but I don't suppose the Navy was paying for it.

The wardroom had a wide and welcoming bar. We were allowed a mess bill and could sign for drinks. These were cheap, and very nearly any drink you could wish for was available. It was all very sociable. At about 12.30 work stopped in all the offices and everyone made straight for the bar. Sherry was the order of the day and we would all buy our rounds. This was accepted practice, for the women as well as the men we were pleased to discover. Perhaps our change of status had brought this about. Four rounds of sherry was the norm before we went in to lunch. I unwisely commented on this in a letter home and got the only letter of reproof I had ever had from my father. He visualised me turning into an alcoholic. I wrote to reassure him.

The Admiral in charge of the Naval Base, to whom we had been to make our number on arrival, was Admiral Sir Harold Burrough, a man of authority who was also humorous and charming. He liked to give the occasional dinner party to which any important visitors passing through Minden, both civilian or service, were invited. These dinners were grand occasions in Admiralty House, which had once been the home of Admiral Doenitz. The table was laid with beautiful glasses and silver and we had very good food. The Admiral liked to have his Wrens well represented. It was a great chance to meet interesting and often famous people and it was here that we experienced that mixture of protocol and bonhomie for which the Navy must be unrivalled.

The rules were quite strict. "Flags", the Admiral's Flag Lieutenant, organised the evening. Derek was typical of the breed, usually chosen for their unobtrusive social skills and their ability to find suitable biblical quotations, when required, for the Admiral's signals. On arrival we were shown upstairs to leave our greatcoats and make any last minute adjustments. We were expected to wear evening dress and I had had to send home urgently to my mother to get her to send me two full-length dresses. We then went down to be greeted by the Admiral and introduced to his guests.

While chatting with whoever you were standing next to - silent appraisal of the room was not appreciated, you were there to do your bit - Flags would mingle, making certain that everyone's glass was charged and showing everyone in turn a plan of the table so that we could find our places without fuss. This "plan" was a flat polished piece of wood in the shape of the table with slots at either side so that tags with names could be inserted. We were only allowed a quick glance, as with twenty or so people he had to get round quite fast, especially as he was not meant to be seen doing this too obviously. Port side, second from end, a foreign-sounding name to my right . . . that was about all there was time for. It was a typical piece of naval organisation: there was none of the "Where are you?", "I'm next to so and so", "Now where am I?" business. We all went on talking to our neighbours and when the steward threw open the doors to the dining-room we manoeuvred to the right place. We would move to sit down as, hopefully, a dinner partner would hold out the chair. At dinner, at one's place, were at least four, usually five, glasses. Sherry was drunk beforehand and sherry also with the soup, then came white and red wines, champagne and usually a liqueur. Some of the invited Wren officers did not drink much or they became verbose and embarrassingly tipsy. After some trials and doubtless tribulations, the number of Wren officers who could hold their drink and didn't lose their equilibrium had been whittled down. These became known as the Admiral's Eleven.

It was an exciting addition to anyone's education. I had never had the chance to attend anything as interesting and informative as these splendid dinner parties. The Admiral's status, second only to Montgomery in Germany, gave him the top social position, unwanted by Montgomery. Admiral Burrough was well suited to play this role. An invitation "to dine" was a royal command. Flags was the organiser. He was also the butt of the Admiral's friendly jokes, but his main duty was to ease his chief's path with deft anticipation and intelligence. To be "Flags" to a great Admiral was the perfect training, I imagine, for the job of Court Equerry. Admiral Burrough's Flag Lieutenant, Derek, fitted the bill exactly.

After dinner it was quite usual to play a game and the Admiral's favourite was horse racing. There was a long "course" unrolled on a table, with model horses attached, which could be operated from one end. Each guest had a horse which had to be wound along furiously. There was some skill in it but not much. Flag's task was to arrange it so that the Admiral won quite often. There were bets and the ladies represented the horses ("damn fine fillies" was inevitably heard). It was quite amusing and made a break from conversation, to which we all returned all the more eagerly afterwards, especially if one's dinner partner was good-looking, amusing or flirtatious. The Admiral himself, in his king-like position, was very gallant and if you were sitting next to him, or dancing with him, his really favourite topic was to tell you about his adored wife and family. With all the wartime tales of unfaithful service personnel it was very heart-warming that he should be such an obviously loving husband after twenty or so years. I wondered if such a prize would ever come my way in the lottery. He gave me hope.

25.

It was an odd situation being in the middle of Germany and unable to meet any German people except the waiters and barmen who looked after us. Fraternisation was frowned upon, even if we had been able to meet a German family and I did not speak German. I would have liked to have asked one of the silent waiters what he thought about Hitler, since anyone with contact with German people was astonished to find that no-one had a good word for him, but it was not a subject I would have dared to broach. The German staff behaved correctly but stiffly, there was never a smile: the tension they were feeling was all too clear. Some of them must have understood English very well and had to put up with our jocular conversation which, inevitably, was quite often anti-German, particularly from those officers who were in direct contact with German officials. Also, everyone was busy "liberating" odds and ends which they had come across in their tours of duty and often talked about this loudly. Almost everyone had got a good camera, either "found" or exchanged for cigarettes, coffee or very little cash. We ourselves had liberated items of stationery that we had discovered in the stores of the factory, including quantities of very good quality writing paper and envelopes. We argued to ourselves that this was our right. A number of less scrupulous folk helped themselves to valuable items, including furniture in the houses to which we had been assigned. Officially, of course, this was very strictly forbidden.

One evening a Viennese orchestra came to the wardroom to play while a large dinner party in the adjoining mess was in progress. At the end of the evening, on request, they played "Tales from the Vienna Woods". It was music from another world, never had I heard it played like this; the musicians' hearts were in the sweeping melody, it was *their* music, a secret precious to them that we could not touch. Their pride, nostalgia and distress was in their playing. I sensed, too, that there was a determination to find a rebirth of all that was great in the

German-speaking nations. It was my first personal step towards losing the wartime propaganda of hatred of all things German.

Being part of an army of occupation has its responsibilities and it was too easy to play the conqueror. Many could not control their desire for revenge. Every individual had his own reaction but it was interesting to see the different approach of the Control Commission from that of the Service personnel who had borne the brunt of the war. Many of the civilians in the Control Commission spoke excellent German and had had contacts and friends in Germany before the war. They also had a cultured understanding of that part of the nation that stood apart from Nazism. Naivety among the less well-educated tended to label all of Germany Nazi.

There was the old cliché about having to show the Germans who was master and there was an odd illustration of this. One RN Captain had the reputation of having a short temper but who was determinedly humane in his dealings with German service personnel. His staff felt that this was misunderstood by the Germans and frequently taken advantage of. One afternoon, the Captain was inspecting ammunition at a large dump which was now being run by German Naval officers under British Navy supervision. The RN Captain wanted to see inside a certain store and asked the German Lieutenant in charge whether there was a light. The Lieutenant replied curtly "No". The Captain pointed to a switch he'd caught sight of and asked "What's that?" The Ober-L replied "a wall", more curtly.

At this the Captain went over the hill and let off the full armament of his rage. He shouted 'Take this man away from me, get him out of my sight, quickly, at once, NOW'. Several senior officers hurried the man away and detained him somewhere until the storm had passed. A short time after this incident, the entire place, we were informed, became exceedingly respectful and the surly behaviour which had been creeping in disappeared.

But we *were* the victors and occasionally the Germans had to be reminded of it. A performance of the Ballet Joos was being put on at the Minden State Theatre and the Admiral had told Flags to get seats for a party of us. Flags was duly informed that no-one could book seats beforehand and that the Admiral must take his turn with the rest. At the dinner, which the Admiral gave beforehand, he was distinctly peeved - with his age and with his rank, Second in Command in the whole of Germany - he expected to be treated by the German manager of the theatre with due pomp and circumstance. However, the matter was quickly sorted out. Two marines were sent ahead to get in to the theatre when the doors opened and keep eight seats for our party. Flags was told that he had got to go without his pudding in order to arrive ahead of us and see that everything was all right. Democracy was all very well in its place but not when the Admiral wished to attend the ballet.

Everyone sent to Germany, it seemed, was going through a trauma of some kind; each one of us had to find a personal solution to the muddle of feelings that actually being there produced. Some found it was easier to stick to wartime hatred, often proclaiming loudly that they could never find it in their hearts to forgive the Germans. There were others who had the vision to see a reformed Germany and a new Europe. Getting rid of wartime feelings against the enemy was a slow business for most us, I suspect, particularly for those of us who had little contact with German people.

My own first step towards a more adult approach came about through catching 'flu. I ran up a temperature and the Medical Officer moved me to a very grand house which served as the Sick Bay for the Base. Here - I think there can't have been any other patients at the time - I was put into a beautiful room on the first floor, full of fine furniture, probably the main bedroom of the house. I was fussed over and had meals brought to me on trays and I read happily for hours. When I felt less feverish I got up and explored the room. In the large mahogany wardrobe, right at the back, I found a very elegant pink silk parasol. It was quite a shock. It so plainly spoke of some feminine and sophisticated lady whose room this must have been, perhaps still was - where was she being forced to live at the moment if, indeed, she was still alive? I held her parasol and thought she must be delightful to have chosen this. It was a first glimpse of what is now so obvious . . . the "enemy" were

154

individuals, breathing, worthwhile human beings, fellow Europeans. We shared centuries of culture . . . this lady's grandmother could have been one of my grandmother's German friends in Stuttgart where she came to study music. What had Hitler done . . . and Kaiser Bill and Bismarck and the lot of them? I put the parasol back into the wardrobe and hoped it would remain unseen and "unliberated", and that its owner would find it there when the normal life in that house was restored.

We were living a rather odd existence. We had no green vegetables at all and not much fruit; there was a panic that we were not getting the right vitamins. Letters were sent home asking for things like black-currant juice to be sent out. I explained to my family that life was topsy-turvy since we had all the luxuries - wine, perfume, champagne, but none of the necessities. I wonder we didn't all get scurvy, but this gives a very clear idea of the state of German agriculture at the time: if we could not get fresh vegetables and fruit as the conquerors, how were the German people surviving?

The social whirl continued. One Sunday I was detailed to attend as a beater for one of the Admiral's shooting parties. Four of us went to Admiralty House mid-morning on a beautiful February day, not too cold and very sunny. Various naval officers were gathering. One or two of them were wearing an amazing collection of clothes. One described himself as a DP - the initials for Displaced Person, of whom there were all too many in Germany at that time. He certainly looked like one. Everyone wore wellington boots, except the Wrens; we just had our Wren shoes, in my case my only rather worn ones as some of my luggage had been held up in Chatham. However, on an Admiral's Shooting Party the state of a Wren officer's pair of shoes plays little part.

When the Admiral came down he was dressed in Canadian battledress given to him by a Canadian staff officer, plus wellington boots. There was a great guffuffle getting everyone into the two cars, one of which was the Admiral's gleaming Rolls. He was exceedingly proud of his Rolls Royce, it had the first automatic window control any of us had seen. It was so new that all of us were allowed turns in pressing the buttons.

We drove quite a long way out to the country beyond the town of Nienburg. One of the Commanders in the party had been made "Captain" for the day and he carefully briefed us all as to the exact duties of a beater. Joan, my upper bunk friend from Hull days, was also on the outing. She had got her commission and had recently joined us in Germany. No-one asked if we would like to take a gun - we were to be beaters and that was that. In view of the fact that Joan had won prizes in shooting competitions in Hull, this was strange to me. She was an absolutely dead-eyed shot - undoubtedly, as we later observed, far more efficient with a gun that most of the male party. However, the possibility that she might like to show her skill was not considered.

When we arrived at the spot previously chosen by the enthusiasts, we all got out and stamped up and down on the melting snow while the guns were got out and everyone prepared for the fray. Then we seemed to tramp for miles and miles. It was very well organised, the Commander keeping us in the picture the whole time by explaining how we were driving the pheasants to a certain place by a stream. We marched along, one gun, one beater, in a straight line across what was now rather marshy land, beating the grass and reeds with a stick and making a sort of "Brrr-Brrp" noise to encourage the unfortunate birds to rise. Much as I disliked the idea of shooting game it was exciting: the absorption of beating rhythmically, making the strange noises in tune with the others, picking our way through ploughland, marsh, woods, regardless of stockings and then, suddenly, a violent flapping of wings as a pheasant rose and sped up into the air, the crack-crack as the gun fired and in a moment the noise was over and the bird was falling heavily to the ground. We had no dogs to do the retrieving so the Marine driver had to collect the "bag". Derek placed the Admiral in the most likely place for a bird to rise. Luckily he did very well, declaring later that it was the best day's shooting he had had for a long time.

About two o'clock we stopped for lunch, returning across the marsh to the road. We sat on the car cushions by the roadway and drank champagne and ate spam sandwiches. Then we had sweet black coffee from someone's flask and chocolate. My shoes by this time were soaked. I considered also that we should have had some commando training beforehand because we had to disregard barbed wire, being assisted over and under it where possible. On one occasion there was no-one to hold up the top wire or press down the bottom rung. I found the only way I could get through was to lie flat on the ground and roll under. There was just enough clearance but it was not ideal treatment for my second best uniform. Our bag at the end was four and a half brace of pheasants, one hare and, sadly, one elegant and velvety deer, which do a lot of harm to the crops, so we were told. We hadn't seen any crops.

We got back at about half past five in the dark and we all had tea, toast and Swiss Roll round the Admiral's fire. What a funny sight we all were, disreputable, rosy-faced, stockings torn in huge splits, all talking about "cover" and "coveys" as if we had been on shooting parties all our lives. The men graciously said that their afternoon's enjoyment could not have been possible but for the valuable work of the beaters. Joan regarded them all with her piercing blue eyes and a twinkly smile.

At the house I tried to dry my shoes out too quickly and they cracked, the soles curling up in horror at the way I had treated them. I would have to see if I could get a pair at the store first thing next morning or I should be giving an imitation of Charlie Chaplin.

26.

For some reason, now forgotten, the head of our section, Commander Nicholas Kempson, had to go to Berlin. There was a free seat in the black Buick and I grabbed at the chance to occupy it. We had had few opportunities to get out of the Base and this was a chance in a million. We set off at 0700 after a hurried breakfast, Nicholas driving, with me in the front seat of the large car.

We drove for mile after mile of tree-lined autobahn, without question part of the finest road system of the day and likely to be one of the few acceptable gifts from Hitler to Germany. The problem was that the scenery, though beautiful, was unchanging and therefore boring. We stopped to have some coffee from a flask. It was a grey day and the forest beside the road was dark and silent.

When I climbed back into the car, Nicholas handed me an enormous pistol.

'We're just coming up to the border of the Russian Zone. So keep that on your lap in case we have any trouble.'

I wondered what sort of trouble he anticipated. Was he expecting me to use his pistol if the Russian guards refused us permission to enter their Zone? I looked at the black stock and longish barrel discreetly. It looked pretty powerful. I had not fired a pistol before but it looked like a two-handed job to me. I thought I should ask him if it was loaded or not, and exactly in what circumstances he wished me to fire it if it was. I also wondered about cocking the thing - it was difficult to see if it had the safety catch on or not. I very much hoped it had. I didn't like to ask any questions and distract him. He seemed to have enough to think about. He was also not the sort of person that one burdened with unnecessary questions at any time.

We left the British border post and drove on a few miles in no-man's land. Then ahead of us was the Russian border post. They had erected a large wooden archway, painted rather crudely in once bright colours which had faded. It reminded me of a well-used billboard for a circus. "Take your seats, Ladies and Gentlemen. You will now see the great Russian Bear . . ."

A guard with a flat cap and a rifle slung over his shoulder stopped us and examined our passes. A bar across the road was guarded by two more soldiers similarly accoutred. The tension increased. Our permission to enter the Russian Zone, through which we had to pass to get to Berlin by road, had had to be signed by both British and Russian authorities. From the way the guard was staring at them I wondered if he could read Russian, let alone English.

'Come on, hurry up,' said Nicholas sharply, not used to being detained by lower ranks. I admired his courage if not his quick temper. The guard looked at him sorrowfully, not understanding the words but comprehending the tone. He went off to his hut to have a comforting word with a superior. Time went by. Nicholas sounded the horn impatiently.

More waiting. Then two guards came out.

Nicholas leant out of the window pointing to his sleeve with his gold stripes.

'Look here, get a move on you two - or do you want me to report you both? I can't hang around here all day.'

The guard reluctantly handed back the passes, saluted and we drove up to the wooden barrier. Very slowly it was raised. With a cheery wave of his hand, Nicholas trod on the accelerator and shot the Buick through. We were out of safe British territory and into an area that was completely foreign - not the Germany we knew. It seemed to me we needed a Russian speaker with us. With "please" and "goodbye" I was not going to be much help.

We continued on a similarly wide road with the fir tree forests on either side, but they had suddenly grown in menace. Who knew if someone would not decide, after all, that we should not have been allowed through the border and send a car after us, or we might be held up en route by a Russian check point or . . .

'Bloody peasants,' Nicholas muttered crossly. 'Keep that gun handy, we may need it. Can you use it?'

'No. But I'll have a go.'

'That's the stuff.'

Nicholas would have liked to have been an actor, as was his sister, Rachel. I guessed that his love of the dramatic was now in full charge.   We tore along the highway at a Silverstone speed.   It was all a bit scary but exciting.   Much more fun than sitting in the Signal Office.

We saw no Russian bears on the endless road; it was just mile after mile of wide, empty autobahn, no other vehicles going in either direction.

We did not wait long at the Berlin checkpoint.   The Russian and British borders were in sight of each other.   With no further incident we were inside the British sector of Berlin.   We drove to a ministry building where a friend of Nicholas's was expecting us.

Had this been Berlin?   I had not seen devastation on this scale since Sevastopol.   We drove down the Unten den Linden but where were the famous buildings?   They had been completely destroyed.   There were piles of rubble on either side of the street, stretching as far as we could see.   It looked, and was, a graveyard.

'I must take you to see the Chancellery,' said Nicholas's friend.   It was in the Russian sector, a vast building with not a soul about except a sentry on duty at the Bunker where Hitler retreated - did a bunk? - for his last days.   It was in the middle of more broken stones, bricks and rubble just outside the Chancellery, which was the only whole building standing in an area of otherwise total destruction.   There were steps leading down to the entrance of the Bunker and we walked down them and tried to open the door.   We wondered what would be left inside.   It was supposed that Hitler had committed suicide but very little had been documented and it was all still a mystery.   The door was locked. Nicholas's friend demanded to see inside.   The sentry refused.   'Niet, niet'.   Nicholas ordered him sharply to open the door.   The sentry shook his head.   Nicholas tried his rank ploy again and threatened the red army soldier with dire consequences if he did not open the door.   But this stalwart wearer of the Red Star was not to be bamboozled and he reiterated, impassionately but stoutly 'Niet'.

We reclimbed the steps of the Bunker and walked over to the Chancellery, picking our way among the debris. Ahead of us were more steps leading to what remained of a balcony under a large colonnade of pillars. We stood for a few moments beneath the columns of the Chancellery and looked down on the area we had just left. Below us was a deserted, devastated area of deep bomb and shell holes, twisted bits of metal and barbed wire and mounds of rubble. The Bunker must have been solidly built very deep below ground to have survived this. The possibility that Hitler had escaped and was living in South America seemed unlikely. We felt sure that he had died like the rat he was, in this trap of his own making.

Soon after the Allies arrived in Berlin, the historian, Hugh Trevor Roper, took over the task of investigating exactly how Hitler had died, interrogating those few witnesses who had not already been arrested and taken to Russia. His theory, now proved correct, was that the Russians, under Stalin's direct orders, removed the charred bodies of Hitler and Eva Braun and destroyed them; at the same time putting up a smoke screen of ignorance about the way they had died. The assumed reason for this was that the Russians feared Hitler would become a martyr, his tomb venerated by his followers down the ages. Exactly what the Russians found, details of the post-mortems, and what they did with the bodies, and the witnesses, have not yet been fully recorded.

The Chancellery was eerie. This was the evil little man's centre of power; how could he have been allowed this power for so long? How had it happened? We went inside. There was no-one about anywhere, it was completely silent except for the noise of our footsteps. We found ourselves at the end of the enormous corridor said to have been specially built to strike awe into whoever came to see the Führer. It was of pinkish marble, with at least a dozen doorways twice the height of the guards, who had had to stand in front of each door on duty. Now there were no guards. There was not another soul in our line of vision. The door at the far end was Hitler's private office.

In the silence, our footsteps along this vast corridor sounded threatening. In my head I heard the echo of jackboots and the violent stamp of guards presenting arms.   We walked towards the open door at the far end which gradually increased in height as we got nearer.   None of our small party spoke. The spectres of the third Reich had us by the throat.

We went in through the impressive doorway.   In front of us was a large high-ceilinged room, not structurally damaged in the Russian bombardment but gone over by those seeking revenge.   We were looking at the remnants of a tyranny.   One enormous silver chandelier was still in place but the other lay fallen at our feet like a twisted monster spider.   Both these chandeliers were of modern design and I thought them ugly.   We felt that there had been no grace, beauty or taste here, only ostentation.   A little man playing at being great.

Hitler's positively giant desk was still in place, too large to move or "liberate";   some of the drawers had been torn out, some broken and everything else movable had gone.   We thought of the Russian army which had got here first.   The Russian soldiers probably helped themselves to whatever they fancied.

Behind Hitler's desk, to the right, was a huge safe door hanging open in just the position it must have swung to when the lock was blown away.   Inside were deep shelves and several small drawers, lined with velvet, which may have contained precious objects.   Did Hitler take some of these objects with him to the Bunker for "safety" or had he left everything here? Whatever had happened nothing was left.   The fortune that safe contained is now unlikely to be discovered - art treasures, precious stones, historical objects - gone with the wind.   Some Russian families might be able to give the answer but do they, in fact, know the true value of what they possess?

We stood in the ruin of this room and thought of power corrupting.   We each of us gave a silent "up yours" to the macabre Adolf.   Over-dramatically, it seems to me now, I remember sending a secret and horrible curse after him on behalf of all the dead, injured and bereaved.   We knew about the camps by then but the full horror had yet to be made public. Our own dead were uppermost in our minds.   After six years of war the

162

gruesome story of Hitler's end, which most of us believed, was some palliative.

'So perish all tyrants,' said Nicholas.

The Chancellery and the Bunker might have been a money-spinner for tour operators down the ages but the Russians thought otherwise. They blew up the Bunker and flattened the Chancellery in the summer of 1946, not so very long after our visit. Nothing much now remains of either.

We were invited to dinner that evening to what had once been Berlin's most famous hotel, the Adler.

'The Adler has been completely destroyed,' someone told us 'you must be thinking of another hotel.'

We drove to the centre and drew up outside a building which looked like one slice of cake remaining after everyone has taken their share. One wall had a door left swinging into space and it was easy to see the outline of where a chimney and three fireplaces on each storey had been. The different shades of paint and wallpaper, charred and streaky, incongruously shared the same wall. Some giant scene shifter had been at work striking this set and gone away in the middle. We parked the car.

Nicholas's German-speaking friend, stationed in Berlin, warned us that we were not going to have much of a meal.

'I want you to see a minor miracle,' he said. 'The whole of the main part of the Adler Hotel has been destroyed. What we are now entering was the staff quarters in the old days. This has now been made into the hotel. You will see fine tablecloths, glass, silver, all the trimmings, but we shall probably eat carrots, which is about all they can get at the moment. However, we shall be served in the same fine style and tradition of what was once a hotel of world renown.'

It was exactly as he said. We were shown by an upright old gentleman in tails to a room about the size of a small bedroom. Here there was only room for five small tables, all laid ready, spotless and sparkling. We sat at a table for four and up came a stooping waiter. He bowed and shook out the damask napkins, spreading them across our laps.   There was one menu only so there was no problem about choice.

We had carrot soup, carrot steaks, a pudding and a savoury and some delicious wine.   We finished with indifferent coffee, which tasted as if it might have been made from acorns.   It would not have been tactful to ask.

We were all playing the accepted roles of pre-war days. The waiters did not appear to resent us.   We were just guests in the hotel who had to be served as they had served many British visitors in the past.   It was a moving performance, a proud piece of enterprise.   It reminded us of their Cockney counterparts who had put up the signs "Bombed Out but Still in Business".   Here it was possibly even more moving, since at that stage of the peace the Berliners had so little of their old world left.   So the Adler Hotel never closed and the economic miracle of German recovery later seemed to us very easy to understand, based rock-like as it was on such individual determination to rebuild their country.

27.

Catherine and I had the chance of a "swan" to Brussels. A swan was a visit anywhere for entertainment and amusement, often disguised by the slender excuse of being ostensibly on duty. Any break in the work routine was welcome. Quite a lot of swanning went on whenever there was the slightest opportunity.

It was our first visit to the city. We looked at all the sights, guide book in hand, thankful that there had been no destruction of the famous square. What we could not believe were the cake shops, filled with mouth-watering patisseries, buttery and cream-filled - such cakes and pastries we had not seen in our lives. We indulged ourselves heartily. Where in the world had they managed to find all that dairy produce?

Catherine had an introduction to a Belgian family, friends of her fiancé's family. We telephoned and were asked to tea.

The Terlinden family lived in a high solid house which they had occupied throughout the war. Upstairs, Madame Terlinden lay on a Louis Quinze sofa in the drawing-room, apologising that she could not get up as she had had a skiing accident. We were made welcome, having our French tested until the family switched to excellent English.

Gradually we heard the story of their wartime experiences. During the German occupation, the Terlinden's two sons had been part of the courageous chain of underground operators who were able to spirit away Allied pilots and other servicemen: those who had managed to escape from prisoner of war camps or those who had been picked up from a parachute landing. These men were hidden and then taken through Belgium into France, passed from guide to guide and taken eventually across the Pyrenees and into Spain. Madame, who was vivacious and attractive, told us a little of what it had been like. Although she spoke lightly, the tension in her face showed clearly the pain of those occupied years, a fearful existence which had ended such a comparatively short time ago.

'I never knew when my sons would be out on a job and how long they would be away from home. We had our precious wireless, well-hidden. The Germans forbade us to listen to the

Allied broadcasts, as you may know, and it was dangerous even to possess a radio. There were often searches of houses without warning and if the Germans found a radio they arrested everyone in the house. But we had to risk it. We listened in secret, it was vital to us.

'What could I do? I had to make sure that there was food available at all hours of the day and night, for I never knew at what time my sons would come in or leave. They often came in at very odd hours.' She smiled at us. We were silent. It seemed this sort of courage required the strongest nerve of all. How many many times she must have wondered if her sons would return at all, or when they were in the house if there would be a sudden pounding on the door . . .

'Jacqueline . . . well, Jacqueline will tell you her story.'

Her daughter, Jacqueline, had been a schoolgirl during the first years of occupation. She and her friends waged their own war of attrition on the Germans.

'We would wait by the swing doors of a department store' she said 'until a German soldier came in sight. Then we would swing round inside, round and round, to try to stop the soldier from entering or leaving the store. It made them very cross.

'Another "game" we played was more dangerous: we would travel by tram at rush hour and have ready lighted cigarettes. The idea was to drop the burning cigarette end into the fur-lined boots of a German officer and get off at the next stop . . .'

Jacqueline had been arrested for one of these "games" and put in prison, still just a schoolgirl.

Not wishing to talk about her war any more, Jacqueline changed the subject. She had just got engaged, a few days before our visit, to a Free French officer. She told us that he had been in the area of the attack nearest to Berchtesgaden, Hitler's mountain eyrie retreat. He and his patrol had been one of the first to reach the rock entrance at the bottom of the mountain. Checking the whole area for booby traps, he suddenly felt one foot catch on something that in the dust and rubble was a little higher than the rest of the ground. Curious, he stooped and picked up what turned out to be a blotter in tooled leather. He dusted it off, opened one flap and saw pieces of writing paper with the letters, printed in gold "Adolf Hitler" in the top left hand corner. He liberated it.

Madame Terlinden gestured to Jacqueline and she went to a bureau and produced the blotter. We looked at it in awe. It can clearly be seen on Hitler's desk in a postcard picture sold before the war in Berchtesgaden. Under the flap were the octavo sheets printed in gold. Under the other flap was a plain piece of paper, torn from an ordinary notepad, with writing: it was a reminder to send flowers to Frau Goebbels for her birthday. At what stage of the war was this note written? Did the Führer have to leave his desk in a hurry because Allied bombers were reported coming in? Was that note the last he wrote in Berchtesgaden?

It seemed to us very right that this bit of enemy spoil should be in the hands of a family who had risked so much to help save so many Allied lives.

At one of the Admiral's larger dinner parties we met a Dutchman who had been one of the leaders of the underground movement in Holland, who recounted, humorously, tales of some remarkably close shaves. As with the Terlinden family, we felt that we could only guess at the horror of living under the German occupation. These people had been brave beyond our understanding.

It was at this same party that the Admiral, in particularly good form, started to tell us about his previous appointment. Before being sent to Germany he had been Flag Officer, Gibraltar.

Noël Coward, whom the Admiral knew quite well, had been asked to entertain the troops in Gibraltar and had stayed a few days with the Admiral. Coward was then due to return to England and he asked the Admiral if there happened to be a ship returning to the UK which would take him back. There was, a cruiser, its name suppressed for the sake of the parties involved. The Captain of the cruiser, Captain X, on being approached by Flags, refused absolutely to give Noël Coward a passage in his ship, saying a number of things about him which were far from complimentary.

The Admiral, hearing this, asked to see the Captain to try to persuade him to change his mind. He added that, of course, as he was in charge of his ship he had the perfect right to decide for himself. The Captain asked whether it was an order that he should take Noël Coward, otherwise he refused. The Admiral stuck to his promise and arrangements were made for Noël Coward to take passage in another ship.

Despite a great deal of tact exercised by the Admiral and by Flags, Noël Coward got to hear of the reason why he could not travel in that particular cruiser. Before he left on the second ship, he handed Flags a scrap of paper on which he had scribbled a poem for Flags to give to the Admiral.

An important point in the story was that the disagreeable captain had once, as a midshipman, had to stand guard over a lot of bodies in some fearful disaster just off the coast of Canada. He apparently got very drunk afterwards and, partly to explain his manner, was rumoured never to have been quite the same again.

The Admiral asked if we would like to hear the poem? There were, of course, choruses of eager assent.

> "Is a stroll among some corpses in the harbour of Quebec?
> In a state of youthful alcoholic tears,
> Sufficient explanation for a soul's disintegration
> In later and more complicated years?
>
> Is the negative achievement of avoiding rock and wreck
> To a nautical but undistinguished mind,
> Enough excuse for being, both unthinking and unseeing
> Unforgetting, unforgiving and unkind?"

The Admiral had most of the poem by heart and said it well until he came to the alliteration of the last lines. There was a desperate pause. Flags gave a perfect example of the tactful side of his job: he timed his prompt exactly - not too eager to jump in, in case the Admiral should recall the words himself, but not leaving it too long to be embarrassing. With the prompt, the Admiral finished it off in fine style. We all applauded. I wrote the poem down from memory afterwards and asked Flags later to check it. He produced the envelope on which Noël Coward had written it.

Also at the dinner party was a Frenchman of medium height and great Gallic charm. On meeting him, greatly to our surprise, he seized the hand of each of us, giving a token kiss and bow. This determined gesture has to be taught young, I later learned, half measures won't do at all. In Spain even small boys from families of a certain class can do the job beautifully. They dart for your hand, bow and kiss, or token kiss, according to age and inclination, and it's all over before us northerners have really had enough time to relish the deed.

The Frenchman was Prince Guy de Polignac, head of the Pommeroy champagne family. In the middle of dinner the Admiral suddenly caused a stop in all the conversations by announcing:

'Well, you're a slow lot. I'm lending my aircraft to fly Guy and Derek to Paris tomorrow and there are two free seats, who . . .' but he did not finish the sentence as I said 'Done,' closely followed by another Wren officer.

The plane would return to Minden in twenty-four hours. We had to square Nicholas over our duty period somehow and get the Chief Wren Officer's permission. Could it be done? It was an unbelievable opportunity . . . we both felt almost suicidal at the thought that we might not be allowed to go.

Nicholas was very obliging: 'No trouble. I'll put off the weekly meeting to Wednesday. Have fun.'

Our delightful Chief Officer, First Officer Harbord, gave her permission with typical flair:

'Yes, you can go, provided you bring me back a bottle of "Quelques Fleurs"'.

28

It was a beautiful morning and at eleven o'clock the two of us set off in a car for the airfield at Buckeburg. On arrival a shock awaited us - the aeroplane had something the matter with it and there would be no chance of flying that day. Flags and Prince Guy understood our distress and stood in the doorway of the airfield waiting-room for several seconds before they dared to come in and tell us of the dreadful disappointment. To alleviate the shock we opened a bottle of champagne that had been brought for lunch on the plane and drank it out of canteen tea-cups. With it we ate our sandwiches. Some of them were paté de foie gras . . . and some were spam.

We reorganised our permission to go if, hopefully, the plane was repaired in time for the next day. Hearing nothing I unpacked my suitcase.

In the middle of the following working morning, Flags telephoned to say we had ten minutes and a car would pick us up. The two of us flew out of the office and raced to our respective houses. I flung a few things into my case again and as I did so, someone knocked at the door to say that there was a car downstairs already waiting for me. I chased down the stairs with my hat in my hand, coat undone, and finished "dressing" in the car. Flags and the Prince were already in the huge black car waiting at Admiralty house. We piled in and the driver let in the clutch. The car shot forward powerfully, gleaming with highly polished black and chromium.

Luckily it was another lovely day, clear and sunny and not too cold. The car radio was tuned to Rachmaninov's 3rd Piano Concerto. At the airport we drove past the saluting sentries to the runway, straight to the silver Expeditor shining brilliantly in the sunshine. We waited in the car while our luggage was loaded on to the plane. There was yet another awful moment of suspense. The pilot pointed out that there were only three seats and we were four. Flags would not hear of either of us going back and volunteered to sit on a couple of suitcases, sitting well forward to distribute the weight since he was not exactly a sylph. We climbed in, still unbelieving, into very comfortable seats upholstered in green leather with head rests.   Very different, I thought, from my first flight to this airfield.   The pilot and co-pilot climbed in with the wireless operator and shut themselves in behind a green door.   The engines were tested and then we taxied forward on to the runway.

The Expeditor was small but of a pleasing design.   As we took off, the Prince wanted to know how much one would cost. Flags told him about five million francs.   He then asked what the next size would cost.

The journey took two and a half hours.   Soon after take-off a bottle of the Prince's own champagne, Pommeroy, was opened. To be flying to Paris in a beautiful silver aeroplane and drinking champagne, I wondered if I could get any nearer to heaven.

We circled Le Bourget airport and came in to an excellent landing although it was snowing slightly.   It must have been snowing quite heavily in Paris because we could see a layer of fairly deep snow covering everything.   Getting out of the plane we simply forgot about our luggage in the regal manner that seemed to be the order of the day.   At the other side of the main airport building an Embassy car awaited us.

Prince Guy had asked us to stay in his flat in the Avenue Henri Martin.   All of us, pilot and crew, went up three flights to his apartment.   We entered the drawing-room, a wide light room with a long sofa upholstered in white with green cushions, and several oval-backed chairs also upholstered in white.   By the window was a very fine grand piano.   The Prince told us that the apartment had been taken over during the occupation by a high-ranking German officer.   There were stains on the carpet, rings on the beautiful piano from glasses, and the upholstery at the back of one or two of the chairs had been ripped open: it looked as if it had been done by a bayonet.

'My wife and I were so relieved to find everything else in the apartment much as we had left it that we do not care.   These are just . . . war wounds?   We thought we would find nothing at all.   Many occupied apartments were left empty - vide, vide, vide.'

The Princess de Polignac was out at her Red Cross work but we met her later.   She was very elegant, wearing a beautiful

171

dress designed by her sister, Jeanne Lanvin. Three of their four children were still in New York, where they had been sent for safety. The baby, called Constance, was in the apartment. Aged two, she had beautiful blonde hair. We gave Constance some chocolate which had to be chopped into very small pieces to fit into her tiny mouth.

The Prince said rather disarmingly: 'We called her Constance because we are "constant", you understand?'

I had dreamt of Paris. Hadn't every woman throughout the war? It was *our* city, a place where femininity had been celebrated to the nth degree. I had long got over my British schoolgirl hatred of "foreign" words and some of my mother's passion for all things French had entered my blood. How often we had looked at reproductions of pictures by Watteau, Fragonard, Lancret, Greuze and the exquisite portrait of Madame de Pompadour by Boucher. The eleborate design of her many-tiered dress was amazing, the falling lace at the sleeve seemed the perfect accompaniment to a pretty woman's arms. Her portrait stood for all the extravagance and elegance that we had been denied over the war years. No-one, except a serious historical student, would have reminded us of the poverty and cruelty that existed at the same time. We concentrated on the perfection of a Sèvres vase or an inlaid cabinet by Boule. What we were determined to remember was the age when witty, beautiful women ruled from their salons, when the rich, or the clever, could indulge their talent to encourage art in this great period of artistic achievement.

So starved of beauty were we that things had certainly got out of proportion. When I first found this poem by Austin Dobson, I wept for a lost world.

On a Fan that Belonged to the Marquise de Pompadour.
Chicken-skin, delicate, white,
Painted by Carlo Vanloo,
Loves in a riot of light
Roses and vaporous blue:

Hark to the dainty frou-frou!
Picture above if you can
Eyes that could melt as the dew,
This was the Pompadour's fan!

See how they rise at the sight,
Thronging the Oeil de Boeuf through,
Courtiers as butterflies bright,
Beauties that Fragonard drew,
Talon-rouge, falbale, queue,
Cardinal, Duke - to a man,
Eager to sigh or to sue -
This was the Pompadour's fan!

Ah! but things more than polite
Hung on this toy, voyez-vous!
Matters of state and of might,
Things that great ministers do;
Things that, maybe, overthrew
Those in whose brains they began;
    Here was the sign and the cue -
    This was the Pompadour's fan!

Envoy:

        Where are the secrets it knew?
        Weavings of plot and of plan?
        - But where is the Pompadour, too?
        This was the Pompadour's *Fan*!

How to describe that radiant city which was emerging like
a butterfly from the ugly chrysalis of wartime occupation? Like
a butterfly, Paris was going all out for extravagance and beauty.
The shops were a kind of paradise, the windows everywhere
dressed with romantic and frivolous articles - there were even
huge velvet bows on umbrellas. How they managed to produce
such luxury was a mystery: at home it was still the age of
austerity.

The people shopping were just as intriguing. Hats were high and dramatic, some toppling over with ostrich feathers in amazing colours. That was the first thing we noticed coming towards us - a HAT - and then one looked at the ensemble, elegance never before seen, fitting perfectly into the beauty of the Paris background. There was just one incongruity: shoes were of a very poor quality, with wooden soles; even though they were elegant and made in cheerful colours and strange shapes we saw that they were not worth the money on the price tags.

In the Rue de la Paix we stopped to look at just one very beautiful hat set in the middle of a large window, all by itself, a confection of roses, black straw and tulle. No price. Just for fun we went in to ask the price in our fairly disgraceful French. Madame was delighted that we should like to see her beautiful show piece, which cost a horrid sum. Alas, this was out of our league.

'But I have just the hat for Mademoiselle.' She disappeared behind a curtain and brought out several delicious bits of nonsense.

We tried them on. They looked quite ridiculous above our uniforms. We took off our coats and jackets but we still looked laughable in collar and tie and tulle and feathers.

Madame spied my sling bag, which I had hung on the back of a Marie-Antoinette-type chair. We had brought some coffee with us. We had been told that there was a shortage and prices were high. We had already given some to Prince Guy.

'Euuh?'

Impossible to write down the noise Madame made exactly. She had seen something sticking out of my bag. The noise expressed surprise, immense interest and avarice. She indicated my bag and asked if I wished to exchange the coffee for the hat of my choice.

It seems now that I must have dreamt it, but for a small tin of coffee I emerged from that shop with a hat of white velvet with two egret feathers, one curving upwards, one down in a sweep under the chin. This magical hat later won me a contract to write a book - but that was some way in the future.

In the Place Vendôme we bought perfume.   With great aplomb and terrible cheek we strolled into several houses of haute couture - Patou, Rubenstein, Schiaparelli.   Now I would not have the nerve to waste their time but then we were made welcome.   Our uniforms were our passports, who knew who we were - we might, in a short time, be on their doorstep again to order a trousseau.   They probably suspected full well that we might not - but there it was, we could not be categorised by our clothes - all doors were open to us.

We walked into the Ritz.   The doorman, mentioned in so many memoirs, saluted us.   We will return, we promised him.

Our money was running short.   We had had to change our German marks into francs on the second floor of a little office belonging to Lloyds, where an old man in Dickensian spectacles warned us of the dreadful prices, and how soon the clean, crisp notes he was handing out to us would be gone.

By chance, the next morning, we had an extra hour before we had to return to the airport.   We went back to the same place to change some more marks, found by meticulously searching the bottoms of our bags and pockets.   We wanted to buy something for our hosts in thanks for their hospitality.

In the office, the older man bounced up when he saw us and asked; 'Which of you is Miss Mack?   Ah, I thought I would never be able to trace you.   I gave you a thousand francs too little yesterday.   Many, many apologies.'   He handed me a large 1000 franc note, a gaily-coloured affair, twice the size of a pound note.

Fantastic.   I had bought everything needed for family and friends, certainly not forgetting my passport to Paris: First Officer Harbord's perfume.   After choosing a gift for the Polognacs, I blued all of the remainder on a pair of white chandelier earrings.

Flags had warned us to be at the Pommeroy offices at 12.00 for departure.   It was getting dangerously near this time as the two of us walked quickly up the Champs Élysées over the light snow.   What an avenue, we had not realised its length. The buildings were grey, there had been no fresh paint for a long time, but it seemed intact.   There were not many cars; most of the vehicles were military.

Jean, my companion, waved at an American jeep.   It stopped immediately and we explained our panic.

'Sure,' said the driver obligingly.   We had to climb in.   We also found that we had to balance skilfully as he drove like the furies and his spare wheel next to us was covered in oil.

In Prince Guy's private office a glass of champagne, as ever, was waiting for us.   He had brought a bottle for each of us as a parting present, wrapped in pink paper, which he pushed into our great coat pockets.   How could we begin to thank him?

Also in Prince Guy's office was a very elegant woman, with that high gloss of perfection of hair, make-up and clothes that speaks of time and money.   Flags introduced us.   She was Flags's reason for his "swan" to Paris.   We knew that he wanted to marry her but that her family had forbidden them to meet. Privately I thought it strange that she did not defy her parents; she was not a teenager.   Perhaps we did not know the whole story.   Whatever the story was, we spent most of the return flight trying to help Flags think of a way to kidnap his Princess - she really did have this title.   It all seemed to fit the fairy tale quality of this adventure.   Years later I heard that this particular romance did have a happy ending.

So the trip was over - the Swan of Swans.   We went immediately to the Admiral's house to tell him we were back. He had a circle of friends for tea around a large log fire.   He insisted on ringing for more tea and toast while we told him exactly what had happened, every precious detail.

29

It would be hard now to describe the daily routines at the Naval Headquarters in Minden. I remember that we worked quite hard in our piping hot factory office but what I actually did as I sat at my desk or rushed about on missions to other offices has mostly gone up the spout. Just as well. This inevitably weighs the tale down on the side of frivolity but I am stuck with it. What I remember now are the people, the parties, the excursions, the "swans" and the fun.

When we had to return hospitality, the task at the Naval Headquarters, Minden couldn't have been simpler. We had to give orders to the Chief Steward and choose a menu, which was then printed in the building. The wine chosen was put on our mess bill and we could even request a particular flower arrangement. We were then assigned a long or a small round table at one side of the mess. Small cards were provided and the only effort one made was to write out the seating plan and place the cards at the last moment.

Sometimes it was fun to do the flower arrangements ourselves and in this case, when we could escape from the office, we would dash downstairs and find the flowers often laid ready, with little vases dressed by the right on a small serving table.

Most of the invitees were our fellow officers. We were with the same people all day at work, and then in various social groupings all the evening. In this situation friendship, and often romance, bloomed. We all of us shared the predicament of being insulated from the outside world by our barbed wire compound. It was akin to working with a team on a film; day in, day out with the same faces - sometimes you wanted to seize an axe to them, sometimes, more often, you couldn't imagine a nicer group of people anywhere.

One of our number, a leading light in the Admiral's eleven, was a girl with a cat-like elegance called Bobbine. She had very expensive tastes, luxury was her by-word. She was one of those rare people who can put a spin on a day-to-day existence and produce a magic social merry-go-round. Not content with the easily given parties in our wardroom, attended exclusively by

Naval personnel, Bobbine decided one day to look further afield. She contacted Montgomery's Headquarters and very soon a group of the Field Marshal's ADCs became regular attendants at our parties.

Montgomery had certainly picked some interesting men. They seemed a highly intelligent group, some very good-looking and great fun. They were entirely devoted to the Field Marshal but not to the exclusion of telling some affectionate stories about him. As Montgomery was not one for any parties at all, I think they were glad of the diversions we offered.

Apparently pets seemed to get attached to Montgomery throughout his campaigns: as well as dogs and canaries there was a turkey called Lucy, ducks, geese and pigs. When Monty was in Sicily, someone had given him a peacock. It had a long piece of string attached to its leg to stop it getting away. The ADCs were responsible for looking after this bird and they didn't like it.

Montgomery occupied a villa in Taormina, which was his Headquarters at this stage of the war. When the army had to move on, the wretched bird could not be found. Montgomery finally accepted the fact that the bird was lost, to the great relief of the two John's: John Poston and Johnny Henderson. Someone later reported that they had seen a bird gliding to freedom from the escarpment by the villa, trailing a length of cord behind it. Someone had released it and given it a shove . . . but who? When we asked, there were just smiles all round.

The army frequented a night club, named after 21 Army Group: the 21 Club. It had the requisite tiny floor for intimate dancing, and the band was excellent.

One evening Richard, another of Montgomery's ADCs, came to the Naval Base to collect two of us for a party at the 21 Club. He drew out of his uniform pocket two brown packets and gave one to each of us. Inside was a pair of the most beautiful stockings, for civilian wear, from Switzerland. Richard had had to fly to Switzerland to carry out some mission for Montgomery and the day before had asked if there was anything he could get us. In the same breath we said 'Stockings, please.' But we both hastily added only-if-you-have-time and not-to-bother-really, and we promptly forgot about it. We were really thrown by his remembering; they were more precious then than rubies.

This particular evening was an international affair. We were a group of English army and navy officers, a French Canadian officer, a French girl and a Dutchman who could speak German but very little English. We had a very good meal and the conversation was, out of necessity, in English, French and German. I strove to keep up and decided that my education had not even begun. Sitting mostly dumb at that table I wished I had not wasted my time. The world I wanted to inhabit was international. When I got home I would have to do something about it.

After the meal we moved to a table nearer the dance floor to have coffee. The French girl tried her wings at a little English. She poured the coffee for us and asked each of us in turn:

'Do you sugar?'

This seemed to be a sensible and traditional use of noun as verb and we adopted it.

At midnight the dancing stopped. The night club was only allowed to operate under army control and we were, after all, on duty quite early next morning. The orchestra played 'God Save the King', which seemed right but a little strange standing on German soil and with the members of the orchestra and all the waiters being German. It was rather a routine rendering but they could hardly be expected to put their hearts into it.

It was announced that Admiral Sir Harold Burrough was to leave Minden. On the evening before his official departure, a farewell party was arranged in the wardroom.

Catherine and I raced back to our nursery after work only to find that our fire had gone out, there was no coal and our room was freezing. Someone else had booked the first bath when the gas came on. We groaned and grumbled and had to boil some water to wash in. To improve our tempers and morale we laid out our evening dresses on the bed while waiting for the kettle to boil.

We had inevitably been much longer than usual. Suddenly, there was Bobbine tearing up our stairs to say that Nicholas, who had kindly arranged to collect us, was waiting with the car outside. I was just on the point of doing up my dress. Nicholas did not appreciate being kept waiting, and to arrive *after* the Admiral was like arriving after royalty - not done. I flung everything into my duffle coat pocket, scent, necklace, earrings, comb, lipstick, powder, tied a scarf over my head, donned duffle coat and hurled myself out of the door, only to realise with a loud shriek that I had left the belt of my dress on the bed. I grabbed it and tore down the stairs behind Catherine. Nicholas was pretending to be in a fury, marching up and down with his hands locked behind him like an infuriated captain on the bridge. We bundled into the Humber and Nicholas drove off. Of course we were not the last and the Admiral had not yet arrived.

Catherine and I went to the comfortable Wrens' room and finished dressing in comfort. The room smelt deliciously of a number of lovely scents. People drifted in and out, leaving a new fragrance in a trail behind them. I clipped on my new earrings from Paris and added my contribution to the bouquet of perfumes.

The wardroom was looking magnificently en fête with balloons hanging at intervals from the ceiling, and with the partitions taken down between the wardroom and mess it had become four times the size. All the chairs had been cleared to the sides and on the other side of the dance floor could be seen one huge table, festively laid.

At about eight o'clock we crowded in to dinner. The food had been specially sent from Denmark for the occasion - smoked salmon, soup, roast turkey, chip potatoes and . . . amazing to us . . . Brussel sprouts. There was a marvellous icecream and a cheese savoury. I hoped no-one would betray us to a newspaper; even though it was a special occasion it was easy to visualise the embarrassing headline: "Navy entertains on Huge Scale while Germany Starves".

There were about a hundred and fifty of us and we drank champagne throughout the meal. When coffee was served, the Mess President got up and made a very good speech of farewell to the Admiral from all of us. Then, to very warm applause, the Admiral rose and made a splendid speech. We all of us liked and respected him. He managed to balance being a fiercely efficient and exigent chief with a friendly and fatherly concern for his charges. The part of his speech which praised "his" Wrens was so phrased that we all felt we had been given a medal.

After the speeches and cheers the dancing began. It was a memorable evening, ending with a buffet supper much later, hams, tongues, more turkey, Russian salad and etcetera. Alas, no more Brussel sprouts.

Next morning Catherine discovered that a chart showing the state of the command, with the names and titles of everyone holding office, was only half finished. This was very nearly a disaster as the chart had to be ready that morning to be handed over to the new Admiral, arriving later that morning. The draughtsman who had been given the job had started it and then been demobilised. He had shut the chart away and never told anyone where he had put the key.

We broke into several cupboards, found the chart and Catherine got a Wren writer to work on it. It had to be ready to go down to the Admiral's office at 11.15, on the dot.

At 11.00, as soon as we could escape the office, Catherine and I sped along to see if it was finished and found the Wren only just embarking on the narrow black Indian ink border. We didn't want to fluster her or show our dismay, but with one eye on the clock we both picked up brushes and worked away at it as if our heads would be severed if it was not finished. When it was ready, we unpinned it and just managed to walk to the Admiral's office without breaking into a run, holding it very carefully as it was still wet. It was 11.18 and the new Admiral was arriving at 11.30.

We knocked on the Admiral's door. He was sitting at his desk staring into space.

Catherine said to him 'Sir, this is a sad occasion.'

'These are the last few minutes I shall sit at this desk,' he said.

We said goodbye and hugged him. It was very emotional. We felt his going to be a personal loss.

There was to be a handover ceremony. Catherine and I raced up to the next floor into an empty office which had a view of the quarter-deck - a concrete courtyard - to watch the ceremony.

The Marines were lined up, also all the heads of departments waiting to be presented to the new Admiral. In just a few moments, on the absolute dot of 11.30, a Rolls appeared flying the vice Admiral's flag and out came Vice Admiral Sir Harold Walker, the Chief of Staff and the Flag Lieutenant. The "Alert" sounded as he stepped out of his car and everyone stood at the salute. Admiral Walker inspected the Marine Guard and stepped on to the quarter-deck. He then walked slowly down the line of staff officers, stopping to shake hands with each of them. He had lost his left hand at Zeebrugge and had a fine gold hook (it was Captain Hook himself, we thought, but we later learnt that he was always known as "Hooky Walker"). The snowflakes were falling gently but not settling.

A few moments later, after a very brief handover, Admiral Burrough came out. He also inspected the Marines, shook hands with his staff, got into his car and was driven away. His proper farewell was to be at a grand parade the next day.

The next day turned out to be freezing cold. Field Marshal Montgomery was present at the parade as the Senior Officer in Germany. It was a very colourful and well-ordered occasion. So this was the great man of the two-badged black beret whose name would now forever be linked to his great victory at El Alamein. Here was the splendid unpompous debunker of old-style military stuffiness. We were pleased that we knew a little about his personality from behind the scenes.

What we did not know, until Flags told us afterwards, was that Monty's first words to Admiral Burrough when he arrived on the rostrum were; 'Now, tell me, which of those Wrens are Angela and Catherine?' Though he swore it was true, I am afraid Flags was pulling our legs.

30.

It gradually became clear to most of us that to remain in the Service much longer was to become old hat. The mood was now "out" and on to a new life, duty done. More and more people were getting their demobilisation papers, giving their farewell parties and saying goodbye. The feeling of excitement about the world outside the Service spread like a bush blaze. Would our papers never come?

My Order of Release came through in May. With it came a booklet, issued by the Admiralty to the Navy, men and women, on "Release and Resettlement". This was an explanation of our position and rights: "For Your Guidance - What to do on Leaving the Service and How to do it". There was a lot about leave, uniform war gratuity and Post War Credit. Printed in capitals was a friendly warning:

BEWARE OF THE MAN WHO TRIES TO PERSUADE YOU TO PUT YOUR MONEY (gratuity) INTO SOME ATTRACTIVE-SOUNDING SCHEME. SUCH MEN ARE PERSUASIVE AND CONVINCING, IT'S THEIR BUSINESS TO BE AND THEY ARE GOOD AT IT. DO NOT PART WITH YOUR MONEY BEFORE YOU HAVE ASKED THE ADVICE OF SOME INDEPENDENT AND RESPONSIBLE PERSON WHOM YOU KNOW.

We were told how to obtain a civilian Identity Card, Food Ration Book and Clothing Coupons and what to do with them. We were also reminded that our name would be removed from the Service Parliamentary register but automatically included in the Civilian Register for the constituency of our home address.

Most important was the free Vocational Training Scheme.

Catherine and I gave our own joint farewell dinner, said goodbye to everyone and departed with a lot of luggage.

At the Customs bench on arrival in the UK, our officer was without doubt from Scotland.

'What have you got thaire?' he asked us, with a fine puff of air on the 'h' of what

'A few wee things,' I said. I didn't mean to speak with a Scottish accent but it came out involuntarily.

'Are you from the north?' he asked me.

'Aye,' I said.   (It was a 'I've-started-so-I-had-better-finish' situation.)

He was very friendly to us, admired my Paris hat, shrouded in tissue paper, and was just about to chalk us by when we had to stop him.   Behind us on a trolley, wheeled by a patient-looking porter, was a crate of champagne which Catherine was bringing through for her wedding reception, shortly to take place.

'We've not quite finished,' I said.   'There's a tidy bit more.'

'My God,' said the Customs Officer, and took off his coat.

When he heard about the wedding, he cut down the duty to the very minimum.   Catherine, who had been terrified that it would cost a huge amount, was so relieved that she invited him to her wedding on the spot.   He regretfully declined.

That was the end of life in navy blue.   Uniforms got packed away in attics.   In time greatcoats and jackets, with their markings removed, were sent to Oxfam, but for a long time I, and I suspect a lot of others, hid our tricornes away.   I was fiercely fond of mine; it represented at least one achievement, just in case I didn't get any others.   We had originally planned to have a hat ceremony at the end of the war and throw our tricornes into the Thames, but we never did.   So the beautiful three-cornered hat mouldered away until it, too, somehow disappeared.

Now we had to press on with the task of learning a trade and earning our living.   Being a Wren was a good start as it made one adaptable, but "outside" we were not the protected and cosseted species we had been.   First shock: if we travelled anywhere we had to pay for the tickets - there were no magic pieces of paper that took us anywhere in the world.   But we no longer proceeded on duty, where we went was our affair.

The Wrens wisely and generously had devised the Vocational Training Scheme mentioned above.   I might have tried for a university place but it never occurred to me to have a go.   I did what most people seemed to be doing and took a secretarial course, often getting into trouble for being late back after lunch.   There were too many delightful people on leave, or just demobbed, and how could one hurry back to pothooks if lunch at Claridges or the Savoy was offered? We were all indulging in a post-war spree of spending our demob pay in a splendid last extravagance, despite the careful advice, before getting down to "real" life once more.

But it had a serious side. A few demobbed RNVR officers could not adapt easily to civilian life, they had got used to such luxuries as a car and a driver laid on whenever they needed one and it was painful to return to reality. A few came a cropper.

There was a feeling among most of the Wrens I knew that a new and exciting, but probably difficult, life awaited us. Ambition and Competition were the twin "tions" we had to get used to. The great scramble was on. Women were tackling new horizons, as was their right, and the big battle for better pay and more demanding jobs lay ahead. It would be a long battle. In many offices, for more years than necessary, the phrase could still be heard: "We can't have women working here, we'd have to change our ways."

'What ways?'

'Well, for one thing, we'd have to censor our language . . .'

One of the strange things, in those first years after the war, were the attitudes of some women themselves. In one or two places I observed that childish tricks, back-biting, sharpened claws and sheer bad behaviour were rife. It was a real Anna-Maria (of Samuel Whiskers' fame) rat race with the toughest and nastiest often getting the rewards. Gradually a few enlightened personalities broke through and women began to help other women instead of hindering them; giving advice, recommending someone for advancement, passing on vital information - in other words, they adapted to the world of work with a saner and more balanced outlook.

The contrast between those early post-war years in business and now are so great that, with some exceptions of course, most women working today would not appreciate how much prejudice and sheer mean behaviour existed. A lot of these attitudes developed because women felt themselves to be on new territory. They were working in a male dominated world where every other woman was a potential rival. Stilettos were to the fore.

The prejudice against women from men was a different problem; this was very strange at first to us, who had worked in the services alongside men and had got used to it, felt quite relaxed about it and had developed a good working rapport. Our first thought was that a lot of men in the business world were weird, neolithic creatures whose attitudes were scandalously out of date. We hoped they would soon wake up to reality. Unfortunately it took longer than we thought it would. "We can't have a woman doing *that* job: we never have and we won't start now," was their cry. But gradually more and more people joined the battle for equal rights and, in time, achieved some of their goals.

A great break-through came with the "Chauvinist Pig" invention, the funny expressive catch phrase that was taken up everywhere. Of course the battle for equal rights is still on but now, I feel, it is a fairer fight. Undoubtedly all those women from the three Services, and the auxiliary services, bursting upon the employment market in the post-war years played a part. They did their bit to change the pre-war ideas that had got deep-frozen in the male mind. It was not only that they had learnt to take orders, they had also been trained to dare to use their initiative.

Towards the end of 1945, a Naval Captain of some renown begged a group of us, when the war was over, to go back to wearing evening dress to the opera and theatre. He deplored the casual wearing of uniform and day clothes which, in his opinion, spoilt what should be an "occasion".

'All you women should make a determined effort to get back to the days of elegance,' he said.

It seemed a lovely idea. What more splendid aim than to be truly feminine again. And yet . . . I wondered if there was not more between the lines of this request; I had a suspicion he was also implying that we should take up the role of dear, obedient woman-at-home once more. I feared that his vision of pre-war womanhood, charming as it might be, did rather place us like chess pieces on a centuries-old board, where our moves were too clearly defined. I had a suspicion that after serving in one of His Majesty's Forces, some of us had other ideas.